CASS LIBRARY OF AFRICAN STUDIES

GENERAL STUDIES
No. 95

Editorial Adviser: JOHN RALPH WILLIS
Department of History, University of California, Berkeley

NUER CUSTOMS AND FOLK-LORE

NUER CUSTOMS AND FOLK-LORE

by

RAY HUFFMAN

With an Introduction by
D. WESTERMANN

FRANK CASS & CO. LTD.
1970

Published by
FRANK CASS AND COMPANY LIMITED
67 Great Russell Street, London WC1B 3BT
by arrangement with the International African Institute

First published for the International African Institute
by Oxford University Press

First edition	1931
New impression	1970

ISBN 0 7146 2689 9

Printed in Great Britain by Clarke, Doble & Brendon Ltd.
Plymouth and London

INTRODUCTION

THE Nuer are among the less accessible peoples of the Sudan. One of their characteristic features is a marvellous amount of self-content, one might say race-consciousness; unlike so many other Africans, they are delighted with everything that is their own and are almost aloof from the new things that come from abroad. They are slow to appreciate the blessings of European civilization and the benefits arising from an ordered administration of their country. Although this outspoken self-consciousness was bound to lead to conflicts, it must be admitted that the personal qualities of the people that caused these conflicts are of a kind that ought to be cultivated and guided rather than blamed or suppressed.

One consequence of the reserve and seclusion in which the Nuer lived, and partly continue to live, is that comparatively little is known about them. The present book will therefore be welcomed by all interested in the population of the Sudan. It is not, nor does it pretend to be, a complete monograph on the Nuer tribe, but it gives a considerable amount of information, practically all of which is new. The special value of the material presented by Miss Huffman lies in the fact that it is absolutely reliable. The author, who has a thorough practical knowledge of the language, speaks of what she herself has experienced and seen during several years' life and work among the Nuer. Whenever her information is not first hand she says so.

The Nuer people belong to the Nilotic family of tribes, which live in the mainly flat country watered by the

White and the Blue Nile. The northern and southern boundaries of the tribe are about 10° northern latitude (200 miles south of Khartoum) and the north-eastern shores of Lake Victoria respectively.

Most nearly related to the Nuer are the Dinka and Shilluk. The latter have numerous sub-sections, such as the Anuak in the Sobat river system, the Jur south-west of the Bahr-el-Ghazal, the Gang or Acholi north-east of Lake Albert, and the Jaluo (Nilotic Kavirondo, as opposed to the Bantu-speaking Kavirondo) in Uganda and Kenya Colony. Nuer, Dinka, and Shilluk show a distinct linguistic affinity, the Nuer and Dinka languages being closely related. The second main group of Nilotic tribes is represented in the Sudan by the Bari, Latuko, and Dongotono. These, on the other hand, show ethnic linguistic relations to the Masai, Nandi, and kindred tribes.

It is natural that people scattered over so large a territory should differ in appearance and culture, yet with all this they show unmistakable common features in language as well as in their ethnic characteristics. It is worth noting that the Nubian tribes living on the shores of the Nile south of Aswan speak a language related to the Nilotic tongues.

One may assume that the Nilotic people are the result of a symbiosis and miscegenation between an autochthonous negro population and immigrating eastern Hamitic tribes. The Hamitic element, in physical appearance, culture, and language, is stronger in the Bari-Latuko-Dongotono group; they are therefore called Niloto-Hamitic, as opposed to the northern (Dinka-Nuer-Shilluk) Niloto-Sudanic group.

Generally speaking, the Nilotic tribes are tall, rather lean, narrow in the shoulders, their arms and their legs,

INTRODUCTION vii

with thin calves, are long, their hands and feet small. The skin is dark. Men with well-shaped features, thin lips, and noses with high bridges and narrow nostrils are not unfrequently met.

Most of the men are fierce, proud, and even haughty in aspect. The Nuer are essentially pastoral; some kind of farming is done, fishing and hunting are also common, but the only occupation worthy of a man is to look after his cattle. The attachment of a man to his cows and of a boy to the bull with which his father presents him may almost be called religious. The one real sport for men is fighting, or cattle raiding, which is practically the same thing. These predatory expeditions are carried on wherever opportunity offers and are a cause of constant friction among the tribes. In their folk-lore tales a favourite subject is the story of cattle fights.

The main groups of the Nuer and the districts in which they live are:[1]

Garjok, Garjak, Jekiang (Nasser District) . 200,000
Lau (Abwong District) 100,000
Gaweir (Fanjak District) 30,000
Lak and Thiang (Zeraf Island, Fanjak District) 40,000
Western Nuer (Yivrol District) . . . 60,000

One group, the Atwot, have partly adopted Dinka as their language.

The Nuer houses lie close to large river systems, so that during the rains a large part of their country is a great swamp, the villages being mostly situated on ridges along the rivers. The chief vegetation is high grass, interspersed with single trees or groups of trees. The country on the upper Sobat, near or in Abyssinia, is however better wooded and has sparse forests.

[1] Cf. Report of the Rejaf Language Conference 1928, London 1928.

viii INTRODUCTION

Their huts are built with great care and skill. They are cylindrical in form with a conical roof consisting of grass, reeds, or leaves, while the walls are made of mud; and are decidedly superior to the buildings of the Dinka, Anuak, and other kindred tribes. The houses stand in small groups, sometimes only two or three together, the land for cultivation lying immediately around each house.

In the dry season the men leave their villages to seek better pasture in the swampy regions of the country. Here temporary huts of straw are erected for the young men who look after the cattle and milk them. During the night the cattle are driven into large enclosures of thorny trees; a fire of dried cow-dung is constantly kept smouldering, to protect the cattle from the stings of mosquitoes. When the rains begin to fall, about April, the people return to their villages to plant dura.

Very little is known about the religion of the Nuer. Miss Huffman mentions on page 56 some names of their gods, but we learn little as to their significance in the lives and beliefs of the people. While I was studying the Shilluk people in the Sudan in 1910, still another Nuer god, viz. Kot, was mentioned to me by a number of Nuer men whom I had with me for some time. This word Kot occurs in a large number of Nilotic languages, its general meaning is 'rain', but in Nuer it designates a god, the idea of this god being evidently connected with that of rain. To Kot is attributed the creation of the world, as the following report dictated to me by a native Nuer shows:[1]

[1] This record and the following ones were, together with the original Nuer text, first published in my study on the Nuer language in the *Mitteilungen des Seminars für Orientalische Sprachen. Afrikanische Studien*, p. 84 ff. Berlin, 1912.

INTRODUCTION

'When God created the people, he created man, and he created the cow, and dura for the people to eat, and goats to eat. He made a spear and a fish-spear, and a dancing stick, such a one as is wrapped with gold. He made the elephant, giraffe, buffalo, teang, waterbuck, reed-buck and gazelle—the yellow and white one, the pig, the cattle-eating lion and the man-eating lion, the hyena, the leopard, the civet-cat and the fox, the rat, the crocodile and hippopotamus, the fish, turtle and snake, the heglig, nabag and ardeb trees, the talh tree, the deleb palm, the kwar and lwal trees.

'And God said to the men: "You are my children, whom I have created; you are four, this is the Dinka, this is the Shilluk, this is the Nubian, and this man shall rule over you; he has the gun, his name is Cwalcotke, he is also called the Turk. He has no cows, but you shall be caught by him, he shall govern." '

Prayers and sacrifices are offered to Kot on important incidents of life. Here is a prayer for a sick person: 'Oh God, let the man recover, let him become well, that he may get strength again. God, what is this? Leave the sick one with us, let him recover. Return to thine own body. Take thy cow, for she was ordered for the deliverance of souls. It is thee thyself who said thus. Take the cow that she may deliver the soul of the sick one. It is thou who created us, it is the cow that delivers souls. Here is the goat, and the wild cucumber. Let him recover! In what have we wronged? Give us the soul of the sick one. Thou art our father. Why shall we suffer from sickness all days? Give us the soul, we pray thee, our great-grandfather.'

At a burial the following prayer is offered: 'Oh God, why dost thou pursue us? Return thyself, take this thy dead man and go; let him be sufficient, do not look at us again. In what have we failed?' Then a cow is speared, and the chief continues praying: 'Oh God, take thy cow. And you [dead man] turn away, do not look at us again. We will give you your own things, but then leave us alone.' The wife of the deceased is now given to another male member of his family with these words: 'Bear children by her, that their fire may be raised up [that their family may not be extinguished], and their family may be able to manage their own affairs.'

A prayer by the chief for a woman in travail: 'God, what is it? why can the woman not bear? It is thou who has ordered the woman to bear children, that she may create descendants, that the man's family may be preserved.'

An important annual event is the bringing of the cattle across the river, where they find better pasturage. For this the help of the sorcerer is sought. He has to find a propitious day for the transaction and to perform the necessary magic rites. He spends the night before in making witchcraft, and the following morning he prays: 'Oh God, it is thou who said that I should be sorcerer, I should do witchcraft, I should bewitch the crocodile. The cattle has no more grass, let the cattle go across the river that they may graze on yonder shore. Oh God, it is thou who created the cow, that man might be nourished by her, let them swim safely across.' When the cows have been brought to the crossing-place, the sorcerer invokes the river or the spirit presiding over the river: 'Thou river of a certain man, let the cattle go across safely, all of them, let them reach the shore safely, let no one be touched by the crocodile. We are making a bargain.' As a ram is brought, he goes on saying: 'Take it, O river!' The ram's mouth is tied, so he goes to the river with it, and drives it into the water. Now the cattle are driven into the boats and they begin rowing them.

These are but a few glimpses into the religious life of the Nuer. The subject requires careful investigation based on a thorough knowledge of the language and can be carried out only by persons who have the confidence of the natives.

It is well worth while to win this confidence and to study the people intimately. They may at first sight not appear attractive and may not generally be inclined to look upon every white man as a higher being, but Miss Huffman is certainly right in saying that they improve on acquaintance; they reveal to him who lives and works among them noble qualities of which this book gives us some fine examples and which justify the labours of those who strive to help them in finding their way from the old, independent, and unfettered existence to changed conditions of life and to a new outlook.

The information given in this book will be welcome to scientists, but even more it will be of value to the growing number both of missionaries and of administrators who are coming into touch with the Neur.

D. WESTERMANN
Director
International Institute of African Languages and Cultures.

CONTENTS

INTRODUCTION. By D. WESTERMANN   v

I. THE TRIBE—HISTORY AND APPEARANCE   1
Stories of Origin. Appearance and Clothing. Ornaments.

II. RESOURCES OF THE NUER . .   11
Wild Animals and Cattle. The Fishing Season. The Food-supply. The Nuer in Business.

III. FAMILY LIFE IN NUERLAND . .   19
The House and Its Furnishings. The Woman's Day. A Man's Work. The Children. The Nuer Girl in her Home Life

IV. CUTTING THE TRIBAL MARKS . .   29
Details of the Rite. Nuer Class Names

V. COURTSHIP, MARRIAGE, AND THE BABY   36
Preparation and Choice. The Wedding. Customs concerning Marriage. Childbirth and After. The Care of Babies. Twins.

VI. DISEASE, DEATH, AND BURIAL .   47
Diseases and their Remedies. Death and Burial. The Close of the Mourning

VII. SOME NOTES ON RELIGION, SUPERSTITIONS, AND THE MORAL LAW .   56
Nuer Gods. Superstitions. Nuer Law and the Moral Code

CONTENTS

VIII. CHARACTERISTICS, GAMES, AND MEASUREMENTS 62
The Real Nuer. Sense of Community. Poise. Faithfulness. Nuer Games and the Dance. Length and Height

IX. WIDER RELATIONS AND INFLUENCES 71
The Nuer as Neighbours. The Nuer and the Government. The Nuer and the Mission

X. THE NUER LANGUAGE . . . 80
Results of Study. Times, Seasons, Moon, and Stars—Names and Determining Dates. Nuer Greetings

XI. NEUR FOLK-LORE 88
Classification. The Coming of Fire. The Story of Kiir. Lest the Earth should quake. The Words of God and of the People. The Words of a Man. The Story of the Young Wife. The Man and the Crocodile. The Crocodile and the White Fish. The Argument of the Frog and the Ostrich. The Story of the Monkeys. The Lion and the Fox. The Fox and his Mother. The Fox and his Brother Tutluet. Riddles

INDEX 107

LIST OF ILLUSTRATIONS

facing page

1. A Nuer wearing the skin of a wild-cat . . 16
2. A Nuer married woman 16
3. Ornaments 17
4. Essential articles 32
5. Women's garb 33
6. Grass house 48
7. A group in a Nuer village 48
8. Tribal markings on forehead . . . 49
9. A carved gourd 49
10. The end of a wedding talk 64
11. A Nuer woman and her baby . . . 64
12, 13. The Nasser Mission 65

Chapter One

THE TRIBE—HISTORY AND APPEARANCE

THE Nuer tribe are found in the southern part of the Anglo-Egyptian Sudan in the Nasser and Abwong districts and also on the Zeraf island and along the Nile.

At the Rejaf Language Conference in 1928, the Nuer population was estimated as 430,000.

There are a certain number of Nuer who constitute what they call their 'aristocracy'. These are not supposed to intermarry as they are considered as one family. They are called 'dil'. A chief is always a 'dil'.

There are various chiefs in different parts of Nuerland, but their individual domains are not large. The people do not make obeisance before them as other tribesmen do when in the presence of their chief. But they show them respect and preference in many ways. If a chief is among those waiting to go across the river in canoes, he is always accorded a place in the first canoe to go across.

Then there are chiefs of the leopard skin, which position is hereditary. These chiefs wear a leopard skin over the shoulders, which is the insignia of their position and authority.

STORIES OF ORIGIN

The Nuer have a number of stories of their origin in folk-lore tales which are handed down from one generation to another. They have a firm belief in these tales of long ago. 'Would our people lie to us?' they ask.

A very large gourd is supposed to have fallen down from heaven. In it were a spear, a leopard's skin, and a person. This person they call Kiir and he is the father of the first Nuer.

They also tell the following tale about the time when the Nuer first came to the country they now inhabit.

THE TRIBE—HISTORY AND APPEARANCE

The Nuer people came to this country long ago, many, many years ago. In a country far away to the west, over across the Nile, there were many, many people.

Latjor, one of the Nuer chiefs, called his people to accompany him as he wanted to go to a distant country where there were no people.

They started out, travelling eastward. They came to the Nile at a point about ten miles south of the present site of Melut. They had no boats. The river was wide. They did not know how they could get across.

While they waited on the bank, talking the matter over, they saw a large blue heron standing in the middle of the river. They wondered among themselves whether it was standing on an island or on floating grass or possibly on a tree. Latjor, their leader, a tall, fearless man, said he would try to wade out to it and investigate.

He waded in. The water was ankle deep, then knee deep. A little farther on it was waist deep, but he waded clear over to the other side. Then his people were not afraid but crossed over after him.

This fording place is called the Ford of the Blue Heron because the blue heron showed it to them.

Latjor led his people eastward, seeking for a good location until they reached Abyssinia. An epidemic of smallpox killed many of his Nuer. Those who remained returned westward and settled in the uninhabited area through which they had passed. Latjor settled in Dwac which is a village in the Garjiok section. He named the different sections of Nuerland after his sons—Garjak, Garjiok, Lau, Gagwang, Geuwar, and Lak.

APPEARANCE AND CLOTHING

The Nuer man is tall, muscular, straight of back, and clear-eyed. He powders his whole body with ashes made from cow manure until he is a greyish-white. He keeps his hair either cut short or shaved off entirely (possibly a tuft may be left on the top of the head), or he lets it grow long and bleaches it by frequent applications of cow-manure ashes applied wet. While the bleaching process goes on he may dress his hair in various styles with a point at the back or at the front or at both places. When the hair is bleached to a light bronze shade he dusts the ashes out of it and is quite proud of the effect. Long black hair is worn only by medicine men. The Nuer man may continue to adorn his body with ornaments and ashes and will especially do so if he is planning another marriage.

The Nuer usually have clean teeth. They clean them with cow-manure ashes, using a twig the end of which has been chewed into the semblance of a small brush.

Nuer men, possibly because they use ashes so constantly on their bodies, and probably because they do not usually wear clothing, seldom have lice. But the strands of beads worn by women and girls are often infested with them.

The Nuer age early, and both men and women look older than they really are. One would guess some of the older men one meets at between 65 and 70. The Nuer woman usually keeps her erect carriage, but in middle life her flabby breasts, broken teeth, or vacant places where teeth have been pulled out tend to increase the appearance of age.

Clothing is not considered essential by the Nuer man and is not usually worn. He may wear a bright coloured cloth—resembling a red plaid tablecloth, only somewhat more brilliant, he may be satisfied with a piece of the cheap blue cloth that is sold by the Arab merchant, his cloth may be of unbleached muslin, or possibly the District Commissioner has honoured him by giving him a cloth or (if he is a chief) one of the gowns they usually give the chiefs. If he does wear a cloth, he wears it under one arm and knotted over the opposite shoulder. The Nuer appropriates any old cast-off clothing he may find. Sometimes grotesque effects are produced when he appears attired in his new wardrobe.

A man must never appear before his mother-in-law unless he is wearing some kind of a loin-cloth. It may be of skin (Fig. 1) or cloth, but he must have at least a one-piece suit on besides his beads.

A woman after marriage must always wear a loin-cloth of some description. And as she grows older, she usually wears a cloth or sheepskin over the upper part of her body, under one arm and fastened over the opposite shoulder.

The married woman's garb (Figs. 2 and 5) consists of a triangular piece of sheepskin worn over the pubic region, with a larger triangular piece of sheepskin at the back, the two pieces meeting at the waistline at each side but not overlapping to any extent. The lower point of each is longer and narrower than the upper points, terminating in a narrow strip about one or two inches wide. The piece that is worn in front usually has a border of beads sewed on it and may have a small bell hung on the end.

Sometimes a number of little thin strips of sheepskin about eight to ten inches long are fastened together and then worn in front in place of the triangular piece of sheepskin that is usually worn there.

The back part of this garb has a border of beads (from one and one-half to two inches wide) at the waist but not on the sides, unless the woman is quite old, and then she may if she wishes have a border of beads on the sides also. Bells, charms, shells, pendants of any kind, short pieces of cowtails, may be fastened at the waistline on the back part of the married woman's dress.

A Nuer girl, when quite young, begins to carry burdens

THE TRIBE—HISTORY AND APPEARANCE

such as water-jars on her head. This accounts to some extent for the straight, erect bearing of the women and girls. She may have a number of iron anklets—possibly from one to six—on each ankle, the weight of which causes her to throw her feet outward when walking so that the anklets of one leg do not hit the other leg, but her general posture is graceful.

Grass skirts are made by taking the outer bark of a certain tall grass and tearing it into long thin strips. These are then rolled tightly and made into grass skirts by a method of weaving and binding at one side, leaving the other ends loose. Grass skirts are made in two sizes, one—the short one—being from six to ten inches long. The short grass skirt may also be worn as a garment by a married woman, for every married woman must wear a loin-cloth of some description. The long grass skirt reaches from hip to ankle, and is worn as a dance dress. It is made in the same manner as the short skirt, but the longer grass is used for its construction.

The short grass skirt (Fig. 4) is usually worn over the long grass skirt at dances. Sometimes a bead is fastened on the end of each strand of grass in the short grass skirt. Both long and short grass skirts are oiled until they are soft and pliable and a dark brown in appearance. When worn at a dance, short bushy stubs of cowtails are worn around the waist at the back over the grass skirts.

The Nuer girl may or may not wear a cloth, just as it suits her. If she does wear one, it is worn under one arm and knotted over the opposite shoulder. Those living near the Arab settlements may dress somewhat as the Arab women do, or they may wear the dresses the Arab merchants make for sale to them. But no matter how many garments she may possess, the Nuer girl—if unmarried—may discard any or all of them at will.

ORNAMENTS

The Nuer man wears necklaces of many strands of giraffe hair (Fig. 3) which are strung through a large bead. He has a method of knotting the loose ends which is clever and neat and at the same time very firm. Indeed, so firm is it that if one person can get hold of another by this necklace, he may lead him wherever he wants him to go as there is no danger of the knot giving way. Sometimes after the hairs have been made into a firm knot the ends may be left and ornamented by having many bright coloured beads strung on them. A man may wear several of these necklaces with various pendants hung on them (especially if he is unmarried or is thinking of acquiring a second or third wife).

A strand of beads, with probably fifteen to twenty of one colour, then the same number of another colour alternately, may be worn over one shoulder and under the opposite arm, while a similar strand is worn on the other side, the strands crossing at the centre, front and back, and the coloured beads glistening against the dark skin. Strands of beads, a number of one colour alternating with the same number of some contrasting colour, are worn around the waist.

An ivory armlet may be worn just above the elbow, a smaller one may be worn on the other arm just above the elbow, and a third (a small one) on the upper arm several inches above the large ivory armlet, usually on the left arm. But when three ivory armlets are worn it is a sure indication that the man is to be married in the immediate future.

Wristlets made either of brass or wire, pounded into various shapes, are worn. The wristlet may be made of a wire which has been beaten flat and thin, it may have several sharp prongs or possibly it may be made of wire with two sharp prongs several inches in length.

THE TRIBE—HISTORY AND APPEARANCE 7

From forty to fifty brass wire armlets of graduated sizes may be worn on the forearm (Fig. 3). They cover the arm from wrist to elbow. This ornament is usually worn on the left arm. The brass wire is heavy, and when first put on causes the hand to swell and often a sore forms on the arm under the bracelets. The man must hold the arm high in order to relieve it of the pain and weight caused by this ornament. But he wears a ring of brass on the right thumb and frequently rubs the ring up and down the bracelets, enjoying the sound made thereby and causing others to notice his ornament.

In case a sore forms under the bracelets, a certain leaf is put in over it. The man is proud of his ornament, and will endure a good deal of suffering in order to wear it. But that arm is incapacitated for work in many cases until the bracelets are removed.

Boys who have not as yet had the tribal marks cut do not wear the brass bracelets.

A man whose wife expects to be a mother may wear a wristlet of either white and black or red and black or possibly red and white beads alternating one by one. This supposedly keeps him from sores and scratches caused by grass.

A few large wooden beads strung on wire and worn either as anklet or wristlet will keep any one from scratches from grass according to the firm belief of the Nuer.

An armlet which is worn just above the elbow may be made out of the hipbone of a cow. It is cut in a circular shape and a hole is made in the centre while the outer edge is notched.

Small beads made out of ostrich eggshell, cut round with a hole in the centre of each, are strung together, and may be worn as a wristlet, or a strand of them may be wound about the waist or neck.

A strand of beads, one black, one white, or one red, one white alternating, with a larger bead in the centre may be worn as a headband, the larger bead being worn in the centre of the forehead. A headband consisting of a number of round blue disks may also be worn (these are, however, bought from the Arab merchants).

Numerous finger and thumb rings are worn. A wire wrapped around the finger several times, or a ring with one or two long prongs may be stylish.

Styles—even in beads—change. At one time bead girdles were worn by the Nuer men, consisting of as many as one hundred and fifty strands of beads, but that fashion seems to be a thing of the past since 1925.

Nuer of both sexes delight in wearing a string of aluminium hearts around the waist (Fig. 3).

An older woman usually has but few ornaments. When she is married, she gives all her ornaments to her husband's people, who, in return, give her the married woman's dress and such ornaments as they wish to give her. She usually gives many more than she receives. Sometimes the husband may from time to time give her either necklace or bracelets, but more often the decrease in ornaments starts at the time of her marriage. Later on, she may give some of her ornaments to her children or to a relative. One frequently sees the older woman wearing wooden beads, and possibly some of the beads they get from the Arab merchants, but seldom has she giraffe-hair ornaments.

If a woman has only one child she may cut her hair, leaving one little tuft on top of her head, and one on either side, and also one in the centre front and back of her head to indicate this.

The Nuer girl adorns her body with many bead necklaces, iron or brass anklets and wristlets, headbands of

THE TRIBE—HISTORY AND APPEARANCE

beads similar to those worn by the men, strings of beads over each shoulder and under the opposite arm, and many strands around her waist. As she nears the marriageable age she has numerous strands of giraffe hair—with various pendants—about her neck.

She may also bleach her hair and wear brass bracelets on her arm. But she does not wear nearly as many of these brass bracelets as her brother, nor does she wear them as tightly, for no matter how much she may wish for ornaments, she must do her work of pounding the dura and must not incapacitate her arm for that work. None the less, the bracelets give many a girl a sore.

Wristlets are also made of giraffe hair with beads of various colours strung on the various hairs. These are quite pretty and add a bright bit of colour to a girl's arm. She usually wears a spiked bracelet—even the small children wear them—and they are a dangerous weapon when they are angry with one another, and wish to strike.

The Nuer girl has a hole pierced in the centre of her upper lip. She may wear a blade of grass, a flower, or a small stick of wood in it, but usually she wears a nail with the point sticking outward.

The ears of a girl are pierced in from five to seven places along the outer edge. This is done with a sharp-pointed native needle, and then little sticks or straws are worn in the holes in order to keep them open. The ears are frequently very sore and sometimes quite painful and slow in healing after this operation. The ears are usually pierced before the girl is in her teens, part of the holes being pierced at one time, the remainder when the first sores caused by the piercing are well. She often wears bead or grass ornaments in them. But the object of this is that the ears may be ready for the white beads which will be put in them when the girl is married. If she has not already had her ears pierced, her husband or his people may pierce all the places in both ears at once and put in the white beads that are the insignia of her married state. Whether her ears are sore or not, she must wear these white beads that proclaim her married status to all who see her.

Bands of beads may be worn on the upper arm or just below the knee. Sometimes strings of beads several inches in length are attached as pendants.

Feathers are frequently worn in the hair and sometimes in the lowest holes that are pierced in the ears. Sometimes a quill is worn in the upper lip.

A newborn baby is not very old before it is attired in bead anklets, wristlets, or a necklace with charms to keep the evil eye away from the child. A strand of beads around the waist, sometimes with a tiny bell as pendant, may be worn. As the child grows older, if a girl, anklets of wire are put on. Also any little child may be seen with wristlets of wire. Shells or beads may be tied to the hair.

If an only child, the hair may all be cut except five little tufts, one being at top of head, one at each side, and one at the centre back and front.

Wooden beads are also worn by babies. No clothing is worn unless some dress has been received as a gift and donned for special occasions—especially if the donor be present. The mother covers the tiny baby with her cloth if she possesses one.

As the child grows older, he wears more beads, either the wooden beads or those purchased of the merchant. But he wears no giraffe hair until—if a boy—he has the six tribal marks cut. A girl when nearing the age of puberty, or even younger, may begin to wear giraffe hair.

Chapter Two
RESOURCES OF THE NUER
WILD ANIMALS AND CATTLE

WILD animals abound in Nuerland. Lions, leopards, giraffes, buffaloes, elephants, hippos, monkeys are found as well as other species, and also crocodiles, snakes, and scorpions.

Sometimes animals are killed with spears (Fig. 4), sometimes traps are made to catch them. Holes are dug into which they fall and are unable to get out. Men sometimes chase them and drive them toward the trap which they have made. Giraffes may be killed in this way as they cannot run fast, especially if the ground be muddy. Monkeys are safe in Nuerland as a Nuer will not willingly kill them. If a monkey is killed, it will surely rain hard, but if it is killed in the dry season, the weather will only become cloudy.

Probably the largest snake found here is the python. Many of the snakes are deadly poisonous. One is a spitting snake. Another is said to bite and also sting its victim with its tail at the same time, much as a scorpion stings. Another snake, the 'thatut', is said to leave a tooth in the person it bites. The Nuer believe that if a person is once bitten by a 'thatut' no other snake will deign to bite him.

The number of cattle owned by individuals varies in different parts of Nuerland. Those who live along the Nile have many cattle. Those in the Garjak country have more cattle than those near Nasser. In the regions where cattle are more plentiful the number of cattle asked as a marriage price is greater.

Cattle with the wide-spreading long horns are the most desirable. A Nuer is afraid that a cow without horns may turn into a 'Lat' (a combination of ogre and cannibal which figures largely in folk-lore tales. Nuer firmly believe in these Lats and fear them).

Nuer, be they men, women, or children love their cattle; they are the pride of the tribe. The people delight in being among them. When a boy has his tribal marks cut, he assumes an ox name in addition to his own.

The cattle are always supposed to see the new moon one night before the people see it.

If a cow is sick, she is well cared for. Everything possible is done for her so far as the Nuer's knowledge goes. A wasps' nest is soaked in water and the mixture forcibly administered to the cow as a preventive against a certain fever.

A bunch of a certain kind of leaves tied about a cow's neck is supposed to help her if all is not right with her when she has just calved.

Muzzles made out of thorns are fastened on the mouth of a calf when they wish to prevent it from sucking.

The Nuer also have sheep, and numerous dogs may be seen.

During the fishing season when many go to the fishing camps, the Nuer depends upon fish and milk for his food. The cattle are always taken to the fishing camp—for grazing is usually good—hence the milk supply.

THE FISHING SEASON

When the dry season is on, the river falls fast and the Nuer is eager to fish. The rivers are full of fish, great big ones, including the Nile perch and several other large white fish which are specially desired for food. In December and January Nuer with their cattle move from the villages to the fishing camps. They build (Fig. 6) bee-hive-shaped houses—even the walls are of grass.

The women and children sleep in these; the men sleep in the barns, if there are any, or among the cattle.

People under one chief spend the fishing season at the same fishing camp. Old people sometimes remain in the villages, but the younger ones enjoy the companionship of others and the change from the routine village life. It serves the same purpose as our summer trip.

While at the camp, fish are caught by spearing them with a special spear or by a hook and line left out all night as a trout line is sometimes left, or by the use of a fishing net, if any one is fortunate enough to possess one.

Later on, when the river is lower, fish traps are made by placing sticks close together in the river. When fish get into this enclosure they are unable to find the exit and are speared and taken. Nuer sometimes imitate the sound of fish by making a splashing noise in the water with a stick. Other fish gather, as they think, to where their fellows are, and are speared.

If many fish are caught they are dried and taken back to the village for later use, or possibly they are sent back at once to those who have stayed behind. Sometimes fish are not plentiful and then return trips have to be made to the villages to get dura for food.

When the river begins to rise, fishing in the swamps may be continued for a little while. But soon all return to their villages, for as soon as the rains start, hoeing must be done and dura planted. Also, should their permanent village be across the river from the fishing camp, they must take their cattle over the river before it rises so much that the cattle are unable to swim it in safety.

THE FOOD-SUPPLY

The Nuer food-supply is frequently limited in quantity; it is also limited in variety. The foods the Nuer will eat are dura, corn, mutton, beef, the flesh of some wild animals—antelope, gazelle, waterbuck—guinea fowl, fish, crocodile—which is considered a choice food—beans, milk, and sometimes greens. This does not mean that these foods are constantly at hand. The average diet of a Nuer consists of dura, fish, milk, and occasionally meat. This limitation of diet works the greatest hardship for little children and the sick and aged.

A Nuer seldom kills a cow unless one has to be offered as a sacrifice. Sheep are not often primarily killed for food. Wild animals are not often available for they usually must be killed with a gun—and who has a gun? Even guinea fowl are not easily caught.

A Nuer will, generally speaking, not eat wild duck. Eggs are not eaten by men as they are considered effeminate. Milk is likewise not regarded as food for men, but women and children and sick men may drink it. Women refuse to drink milk during their menstrual periods.

The staple article of food is dura, or kaffir corn as we call it. The dura is planted in May, providing the early rains have begun. If the rainy season is late the planting is delayed until the ground has been softened by several rains so that hoeing is possible. Small hand-hoes are used. Everybody hoes—men, women, and children each do their part in getting the field ready to be planted. The seed dura, which has been kept over from the past year, is sown. It requires to be hoed several times during the season, for the frequent rains make weeds grow as well as dura. In late September or early October, according to the time of planting, the dura is ready to be cut.

When harvest time approaches a 'guk kwoth' or 'prophet of god' is consulted as to when they may cut their dura, and his advice is heeded.

RESOURCES OF THE NUER

Every one helps in the work of the harvest, for the stalks must be cut down and the heads cut off and placed upon a rack which has been placed in the yard for that purpose. The grains of dura are pounded out, then it becomes the property of the housewife after the seed dura has been selected and stored for the coming year.

The stalks of dura are often kept for fuel or for making fences.

If the rainy season has started early there may be a second crop of dura, but this seldom happens.

The wife must pound the dura and sift it to get the bran out. She pounds it in a hole in the ground which she has plastered with mud, using a long pole. She usually chants a song as she pounds, the thud of the pounding serving as a low accompaniment to her song.

The dura is cooked like mush and forms the main part of the food of a Nuer. He eats it without salt or sugar; sometimes he has a little milk on it. Or the dura may be soaked and then allowed to sour a little, and then cooked, in order to give the family a little variety in their meals.

Corn is also eaten, usually being parched. They also chew the dura stalk or the sugar-cane stalk (if they have it) for the sugar they find in them.

Some wild tubers are eaten, and some kinds of wild greens. Beans are also eaten, but I know of no Nuer who plants them in his own village. Men consider these wild greens effeminate and will not eat them except in times of famine. Sometimes in times of famine they gather certain wild grass seeds and cook them as a food.

The Nuer is not inclined to plant any large field and thus be assured of a surplus of food. The Arab merchant comes to his village when the dura is threshed and shows such an array of beads and cloths that the Nuer is tempted to part with some of his dura. So want is never far from the door of the Nuer home.

A drink—more or less intoxicating, according to the amount one drinks of it—is made from dura. Nuer are very fond of it. They frequently get intoxicated enough to fight when they have had their fill of it.

THE NUER IN BUSINESS

Few Nuer men engage in any business that helps others. Practically every Nuer man has a plot of ground where he may raise the family's supply of dura, but he seldom thinks of raising any to sell.

The Government has tried to interest the Nuer in raising cotton, but with no marked success so far.

A few men are blacksmiths and make the spears, fishing spears, and ornaments out of iron, brass, or wire. They sharpen old hoes, spears and such like, and make good money in this line. The equipment a blacksmith requires is decidedly meagre. A piece of iron to hammer on, a piece of iron to hammer with, and a fire, constitute the usual equipment, although one occasionally sees a chisel.

Some men make a reputation for themselves by their skill as roofers. The roof of a Nuer house when new is a very pretty piece of work, being quite smooth and even. It takes a good roofer to fix a roof so that the heavy tropical rains do not go through it. Men roof the houses, but the making of the long grass eaves to protect the wall from rain is considered as women's work and is left for them to do.

Women sometimes make earthen pots and sell or trade them to others who are not so well versed in this art, but practically all women are more or less proficient in pottery.

Fig. 2. A Nuer married woman

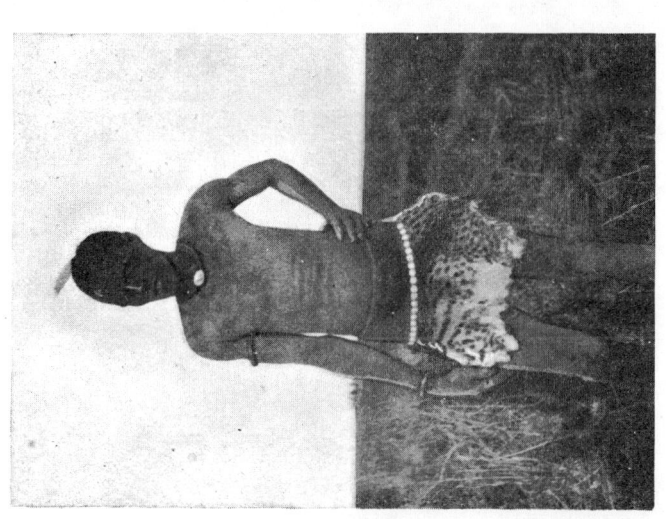

Fig. 1. A Nuer, wearing the skin of a wildcat as a loin-cloth

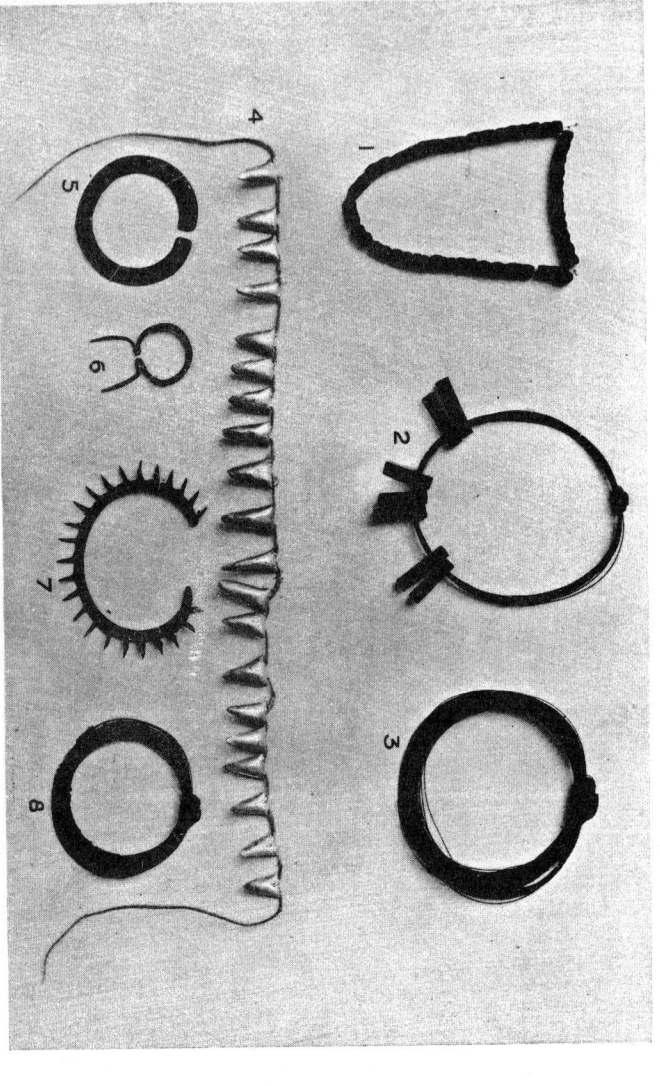

Fig. 3. ORNAMENTS

1. Necklace of wooden beads. 2. Necklace of giraffe hair with wooden pendants. 3. Necklace of giraffe hair (note the knot). 4. Aluminium ornaments worn around waist. 5. Wristlet of brass wire, pounded flat. 6. Two-pronged wristlet. 7. Many-pronged wristlet. 8. Wristlet of giraffe hair with beads

RESOURCES OF THE NUER

Many Nuer find work near the Arab settlements, or at the mission. But the work that they do at these places is different from what they have done in their tribal life. Wages for a man who works—or should work, but often does not—six hours a day range from fifty piastres to £1 per month, plus five piastres additional each week for food. This is the wage given at one mission. (The wages given are approximately equivalent to $2.50 to $5 per month, plus 25 cents. per week for food.) Wages are based upon the kind of work done. Those working for the Arabs near this same mission do not get as much. Girls who work in the Arab homes frequently get gifts of food.

Some boys receive higher wages than this for special kinds of work which they have been trained to do.

In one mission some boys have learned to do quite accurate work on the multigraph, others have developed into good teachers, showing remarkable ability, while a few have shown that they have talent which could be used in public speaking or preaching.

Some of the houseboys have developed into splendid cooks, being able to read a menu written in Nuer and prepare the meal desired without help. A number also can bake bread.

The District Commissioners use interpreters who can write, and are finding more use for boys who have had some school training.

Occasionally some Nuer fell a tree, cutting the trunk to the length required for a canoe. Then they will hollow it out and make a canoe of it.

All this goes to prove that the Nuer has latent powers which are capable of accomplishing much if rightly developed. It must be admitted that there are Nuer—or at least one—whose mind periodically turns toward evolving a plan for higher wages, and he succeeds in getting others to quit work with him and await an increase in wages.

Thus one is brought face to face with the fact that the first result of education, even in Nuerland, is to bring out what is latent in heart and mind.

Chapter Three

FAMILY LIFE IN NUERLAND

THE HOUSE AND ITS FURNISHINGS

THE Nuer does not live to himself. He is a part of his particular village, and his actions affect all his relatives, no matter how distant the relationship may be. This fact checks him to some extent in his misdeeds, for any infringement of Nuer law not only affects him but all his people as well. He must give heed to them and to Nuer law in general if he is to count on their support and aid in time of need (Fig. 7).

The men and boys of the village usually sleep in the barn which is to be found in most villages. A house is set aside for the sleeping quarters of the girls. The women and little children sleep in the houses.

The Nuer house is conical in shape. It has mud walls up to about three feet or more from the ground, then the sloping grass roof. There are no windows. A door, woven like a mat, is made of grass. If the weather is cool, a fire is made inside the house and the smoke goes out through the roof. At night the door is tightly closed in order to keep wild animals out, so the ventilation is indeed poor.

A fence of cane-stalks is made and encloses a small yard. The door of this fence as well as the door of the house are made low so that one must stoop in order to get in.

The yard is swept clean—a bunch of grass tightly tied together at one end suffices for a broom. One part of the enclosure is plastered with mud for a radius of two or three feet, and in the centre is a hole, also plastered, in which the women may be found pounding the dura, making use of a long pole. The dura is pounded very fine, the coarser parts being sifted out by shaking it on a grass tray. The dura can be pounded as fine as flour, but that involves much physical labour. The woman frequently chants a song as she pounds.

The household furnishings vary in number, but in most of the average homes the following articles which are considered necessary (Fig. 4) by the Nuer are to be found.

A large earthen vessel for carrying water.

An earthen cooking-pot.

A long-necked gourd having a small hole in the end of the neck. This is used as a milk-pail; milk may also be churned in it by taking hold of the neck and shaking the gourd vigorously to and fro.

Several half-gourds of various sizes which are used as dishes for food; the smaller ones may be used as drinking cups.

A number of mussel shells for use as spoons. Spoons are also made of the horn of the antelope.

A clay pipe with a long stem—this is much in evidence.

A large earthen container for dura (kaffir corn).

Network bags made out of grass rope. These are used to hold gourds of various sizes.

A large basket, woven in openwork pattern, to hold various possessions when travelling.

A spear and a fishing spear.

A big-headed club, and also smaller clubs.

A ring made of cane-leaves is used as a pillow by the women. The pillow for men is made out of a piece of a tree and has three legs. Part of a tree is chosen where the branches fork in the desired direction.

A baby basket woven of a certain pliable kind of wood, and also a grass mat to cover it with.

Skins of sheep are used as rugs to sit on, and the skin of the waterbuck makes an ideal bed.

A fire, with earthen shield to protect it from the wind,

occupies a place in the enclosure. Cane-stalks are generally used for fuel, although the women may go to the forest and bring wood.)

The skin of a reed-buck is not usually seen in the Nuer home. A Nuer woman whose first child is a girl will not sit on the skin of the reed-buck as she believes sores will break out on her body if she does so. So the skin of the reed-buck is not as popular as it might be if there were no superstition attached to it. I gave a woman guest the skin of a reed-buck to sit on one day—thinking that I was honouring her, for it certainly was pretty—and was amazed at the way she suddenly sprang to her feet and got off the skin, explaining her actions by saying that her first child was a girl.

A visitor—if a stranger in Nuerland—is appalled by the paucity of the possessions in a Nuer family. What they have seems, even at its best, such a meagre portion of the things we think necessary for this life. Yet the wants of the Nuer are few. He wants food, a place to sleep in, cattle, at least one wife and as many more as he can possibly afford, and children. He wants also a good spear and club. These desires of his heart he wants to have supplied with the least possible effort on his own part.

THE WOMAN'S DAY

The day begins early for the mother. Soon after daybreak she must take her large earthen jar and go to the river for water. She has a head-pad made of cane-leaves, with a hole in the middle of it—indeed, it resembles a huge doughnut. She puts this head-pad on her head and then puts the large earthen jar on top of it. She carries herself erect, occasionally putting one hand up to steady the jar. But usually she lets one hand hang down while in the other she carries her long-stemmed pipe, smoking as she goes. She steadies her jar with her hand as she goes down the river bank.

She rinses her jar with water, then fills it. She usually stops to wash her face and is then ready to return to her village. She calls one of the other women who are getting water, or if there are none there to help she calls some passer-by, who—even if it be a man—will usually stop to help her to lift the jar up and put it on her head. On the homeward trip she steadies the jar with one hand, as being full of water it is much heavier.

When she returns to her home the morning meal must be ready by nine or ten o'clock. So she pounds the dura in the hole already described, and sifts it until she has enough for the morning meal. Or perhaps she has a large stone, in which case she takes a small piece of smoothed wood resembling our rolling-pin and grinds the dura on the stone with it.

Then the fire is built with cane-stalks for fuel, and the earthen cooking-pot, partly filled with water, is put over the fire. It is supported by three little mounds of hard baked earth, and she keeps shoving the stalks of cane into the fire as fast as they burn away. The pounded dura is put into the water gradually, a little at a time, and stirred frequently with a cane-stalk having two small cross-pieces fastened at right angles at the end of it, made for that purpose. When the food is ready, the woman dishes up the men's portion in a large half-gourd which serves as a dish, puts the mussel-shell spoons in it, and calls the men to their breakfast. They go into the house and eat.

Then the women, if they are young or newly married, eat where they will not be seen by the men. If they have been married several years they may eat together.

The yard has to be swept, the children fed and cared for, more dura must be pounded for the evening meal.

FAMILY LIFE IN NUERLAND 23

If there are cattle to be milked, the woman must milk them morning and evening. In the afternoon she must again go to the river to refill the water-jar. She usually stops to bathe if she comes from any distance.

Sometimes this work of getting the water-jars filled twice a day is not as merely routine as it sounds; it may be fraught with danger in this crocodile infested river. One afternoon about five o'clock, a huge crocodile was seen sunning itself on the river bank right in the path down which the women would come to get water between five and six o'clock.

The bank was steep, no one could possibly see the crocodile until he started down the slope. Then it would be practically impossible to get away until too late, because the woman would be burdened with her heavy water-jar, and that, together with the steep bank and her surprise at finding the crocodile there, would retard her escape.

But a missionary was passing in the launch and saw the crocodile. He realized its purpose, but not in time to shoot as he went by. But the launch quickly circled around again and slowly approached the path where the crocodile lay awaiting its prey. He shot the top of its head off; it gave one shudder and then never moved from its place. The Nuer in the launch wanted the meat, for crocodile tail in their estimation makes delicious steak. But one of the women missionaries in the launch objected seriously when the men wanted to cut off the crocodile's tail. She wanted to be sure it was dead, so that there would be no possible chance of any objections from the crocodile to the tail-amputation affair. The men did not seem to feel that a crocodile with the top of its head blown off would have much power to object to anything that might be done to it. But to appease feminine fears the pistol was brought and another bullet was fired into the lifeless body of the victim.

One wonders what happened during the next hour when the women came to fill their water-jars. What would their thoughts be as they stepped down the river bank and at a turn in the path encountered the brainless, tailless body of a huge crocodile? Would they think of the dreadful fate from which they had been saved, just because a launch happened to pass that way a few minutes before, or would they grieve because the choicest steak had already been taken?

The woman has the bulk of the work, but she seems to expect it. When the day's toil is over, the dura pounded, the two meals cooked, the water carried, the children cared for, the mother sits there in the light of the smudge fire which is made to keep mosquitoes away. She has had a busy day. Now they all sit around in the firelight, visiting, or telling tales of long ago, or maybe they are telling riddles. Some one may be strumming a native-made stringed musical instrument, another may be singing, and yet the conversation goes on uninterruptedly. If in the light of the moon, bedtime does not come early—probably not until ten or twelve o'clock or later—but if it is in the dark of the moon, they seek sleep earlier and nine or ten o'clock finds the village quiet. Another day is past, the woman is in her home, her children about her, her husband satisfied with his food for the day and happy with her. What more could she wish?

The baby must be cared for during the day and taken up and nursed every time it cries. The Nuer baby is nursed until it is at least two years of age, and more often until it is three or even four. They have a superstition that usually keeps the husband and wife from having another child while a child is not yet weaned. Water must be heated in the late afternoon for the baby's bath. It is no short process. (Fig. 11)

A MAN'S WORK

A man's work usually begins at sunrise too. He has probably slept in the barn. He arises, covered with cow-manure ashes. He cleans his teeth with the ash and later on in the morning may wash his face and hands. While he may drink a large quantity of water during the day he seldom drinks any water before breakfast or with a meal. He usually stays among the cattle until he is called to his breakfast about nine o'clock. Then he eats and is ready to spend the day among the cattle. He takes them out to graze about ten o'clock in the morning and returns with them in the late afternoon. He loves his cattle. His day is a happy one spent in their midst, his human companions being other men who have taken their cattle out to graze also. His spear and club are ever with him. In the late afternoon he comes home with his cattle, finding his supper is being prepared. A plunge in the river every time he goes to it refreshes him. After supper is over visiting until bedtime is the usual close of the work of the average day.

The day's work may be varied if any of his cattle are sick or if there is a dance which he wishes to attend. Or maybe the District Commissioner is in the village hearing cases or collecting taxes, and so he joins the throng and spends his day listening to the cases or bringing up some case of his own before this representative of the Government. During the planting season, the fishing season, or the season when the dura must be cut, this daily programme of the Nuer man differs and his work for the day may be a little more strenuous.

THE CHILDREN

The little children of the village spend their day in play, eating, and sleeping. The babies are often cared for by the grandmothers. The older children are called on to carry water or to help in some way. The older girl helps her mother in the routine duties of the day.

The little boy in the home plays games. He may have a cane-stalk and string for a fishing-rod and line, and sometimes a bent pin for a hook. When he is about eight years old he begins to herd the sheep each day. He often makes men and cattle out of mud and plays with them.

When he is old enough to have the tribal marks cut, his status is at once changed from that of boy to man. His privileges are also increased. He is now interested in securing cattle and sheep of his own.

The children love their folk-lore tales and the many animal stories that are told them by their elders. They believe these implicitly and fear the dreadful ogre that is usually the central figure of the story. They also amuse themselves by guessing riddles, of which they have a large number.

But while they are learning many things that are interesting and useful, they are learning many things they do not need to know. They learn to curse. They learn indecency in regard to sexual matters. Indeed, the child mind is full of many things that pollute both thoughts and actions. The lack of privacy in the village and family life account for much of this pollution of mind and action which infests the child. And there is no decidedly corrective method used by the elders of the village. Life was always so, it always will be so, they think.

THE NUER GIRL IN HER HOME LIFE

The life of a girl in the Nuer home is a foretaste of the life of the mother. The bulk of the work which can be done by the children falls to her. When just a little girl she must take a gourd and carry water, learning to balance it on her head. She must help to care for the baby, carrying it astride one hip, with her arm around it. Cane-stalks must be brought for fuel, or she may accompany her mother when she goes to the forest to get wood. She gathers sticks of wood, binding them together with grass, and carries them home on her head. Or she may accompany her mother when she goes out to cut grass for roofing the houses. She early learns to carry her burden poised on top of her head.

As she grows older she learns to pound dura and to sift and cook it. She learns all the art of the Nuer housekeeper and, indeed, soon becomes a small replica of her mother.

The little girls play 'keeping house' and imitate their mothers to the best of their ability.

The older girls of the village usually have a house given them for sleeping quarters.

As the girl grows older she learns to smoke the family pipe and becomes as attached to it as her mother is.

When she is twelve or thirteen years old she begins to observe the age-old customs which until then she has been able to ignore. For instance, now she must never eat before a boy of her own age or older. Furthermore, she must never see him eat if there is any possibility that he may some day be a suitor for her hand in marriage.

She bleaches her hair and adorns her body with all possible ornaments. She dons her grass skirts and attends dances now. Her father and brothers are interested in giving her beads and other ornaments, for a well-favoured girl will bring more cattle when the marriage price is discussed. Her father and brothers are dictators as to what she may do and as to what plans may be made for her future. She must do as they say or pay for her refusal by beatings from them. Her lot is not a pleasant one if her desires conflict with the plans of her father or brothers.

If she has been a victim of that dreadful tropical disease, yaws, and has any ulcer caused by it, her brothers may take her to the nearest medical aid—either to the Government or mission clinic—and seek healing for her, for they will be at a decided disadvantage in obtaining the marriage price they seek if their sister is still suffering from this disease and has unhealed ulcers.

Or she may have trachoma and may have suffered for years from trichiasis, and now they seek medical and surgical aid for this. What man will want a half-blind wife or be willing to pay any reasonable number of cattle for her? But when these physical defects are remedied, they may hope to get the usual number of cattle for her, and that, to them, is the major point.

Their sister must be physically able to bear a living, healthy child and regain her own health. Or, if she fail repeatedly in the first point or possibly fails to survive the ordeal of child-birth herself, her husband and his people may, and practically always do, ask for the return of the cattle which they paid as the marriage price.

So it is worth their while to invest the price of a sheep or two in securing physical health for their sister in order that she may bring them a greater number of cattle, and that her physical condition may not cause them to have to return the cattle they have received for her.

Her lot may be a most unhappy one if the man she loves has not the number of cattle her people desire or if they wish her to marry some one else. But if her health is good and her desires in regard to her future husband coincide with those of her family, her lot is a happy one.

Chapter Four

CUTTING THE TRIBAL MARKS

DETAILS OF THE RITE

BY far the most important event in the life of a Nuer boy comes when he has about reached the age of puberty. His people decide that he must have the tribal marks (Fig. 8) cut when the cold winds blow. He knows that now, at least for a short time, he will be the centre of attraction in his village. The younger boys follow after him; he enjoys their admiration and envy.

He has his hair shaved off, not a spear of hair must be left. He removes all his clothing, if he has any, and beads. Ornaments of all kinds, every one of them, must be discarded.

Some men are known to be expert at cutting the tribal marks and they are much in demand as the season of cold winds approaches, for each year there are usually boys in each locality who must have the tribal marks cut and the services of some one who is an adept at the work is required.

Usually this rite is executed upon several boys at the same time and place, so that they may find companionship in the company of each other while they recuperate from this dreadful ordeal. For ordeal it is, no matter how much they try to bolster up their courage.

The boys are allotted a house in which to sleep the night before this rite takes place. Sometimes they secure the kind of pillow which is used by Nuer women, a ring of cane-leaves having a hole in the centre. They practice sleeping on it, for they must use that kind of a pillow until their wounds heal.

The night passes, but little sleeping is done. Before daybreak the people are stirring, for the man who will cut the tribal marks comes at or before sunrise in order that the ordeal may be over and the boys safely back in the house before the heat of the day begins.

The boys remain in the house, awaiting their call, so that no one with the evil eye may see them.

The girl friends of the boys are also *en route* before sunrise, so that they may see how bravely the boys act when suffering so intensely. The women of the village don their long grass dancing skirts.

A hole from four to six inches in diameter and about six or eight inches deep is dug for each boy. The earth which is taken out of the hole is pulverized and spread around the hole in order that it may absorb the blood. Women and girls attired in their dance skirts rush in, singing and dancing.

One boy is called. He comes out, stark naked, not even wearing a bead. He lies down on his back with his head in the hole. He folds his arms over his chest and then he is ready.

The man, kneeling beside him, begins to cut. He starts at the centre of the forehead and extends the cut to or even past the ear. The first cut is made just above the eyes, then the remaining cuts are made parallel to it until they are six in number. Then the man goes over to the left side and, kneeling there, repeats the same process. Then he returns to the right side and makes sure that all of the cuts are deep and continuous at the centre of the forehead, and that they are six in number.

The boy usually lies absolutely still, for a show of fear on his part would bring ridicule from the girls and women that would be hard to bear, and if he moves it will mean that the cut will not be straight and he will always have to wear a scar that will proclaim to any Nuer that he flinched while the tribal marks were being cut.

As one is finished another boy is called until all lie there, still and bleeding. Usually everything is very quiet when the actual cutting is going on, the only sound heard being the grating of the knife upon the bone.

The boy lies there until the bleeding has stopped, then he is helped into the house. He crawls into the house on his hands and feet, but with his back next to the ground and tries to hold his head and body in a horizontal position. The man who cuts these tribal marks is supposed to stay for a while if he can, in case there should be haemorrhage.

If there should be haemorrhage, pressure and the application of cow-manure ash is tried to relieve it. Also fear is expressed that some one with the evil eye must have seen the boy or else there would have been no haemorrhage.

Soon after the tribal marks are cut a sheep is sacrificed in order to insure safe healing of the cuts. A little later a mock fight is staged between the men and the women of the village in which the women are allowed to use clubs, but the men must defend themselves bare-handed.

The boy is carefully guarded against the evil eye. He wears a piece of sheepskin over his head, this piece of sheepskin usually being one part, the back section, of a married woman's garb which has been given for this purpose. No one is supposed to view the cuts until they are healed, but the boy usually gives some trusted friend an opportunity to see them.

After some days the cuts are washed, but not immediately, for the clotted blood is left undisturbed for some time.

The boy usually carries a large cluster of feathers as a fan in order to keep the flies away from his head.

He is the centre of attraction at his village now. All visitors to the village are met at a little distance and their names announced before they may come near, for the evil eye must constantly be guarded against.

An animal skin is always spread on the ground for him to sit on. Food is specially prepared for him in order that he may speedily regain his strength and vigour again. He is treated as a most honoured guest in the village, and is the centre of concern.

Later on the boy is supposed to give some gift to the man who cut the tribal marks for him. Sometimes this man happens to be a very dear friend of the boy and may honour him by cutting seven cuts instead of the customary six.

The boy takes cane-stalks and peels them, cutting them into four-inch lengths. He makes a girdle or belt of them by fastening them together side by side. He may go visiting at night after his wounds are well on the way to recovery, and he always wears this belt. He also carries a long stick which has a piece of ambatch or other light wood at the end of it, and also a cluster of white feathers.

He is not allowed to go among the cattle until he is entirely well. When one asks him if his wounds are healed he will always say 'not yet', but one may find out if they are really healed by asking him if he has gone among the cattle. If not, the wounds are still sore, but if he has been with the cattle it means that the wounds are well healed, although the boy will not say so for fear some one with the evil eye should hear of it.

No pregnant woman must come near the boy until his wounds are healed; a man whose wife is pregnant must also be avoided.

Nuers do not wear bead necklaces after the tribal marks are cut, although strands of beads may be worn around the waist or over each shoulder and under the opposite arm. Wooden beads may be worn for a few months, then they may wear the giraffe hair necklaces.

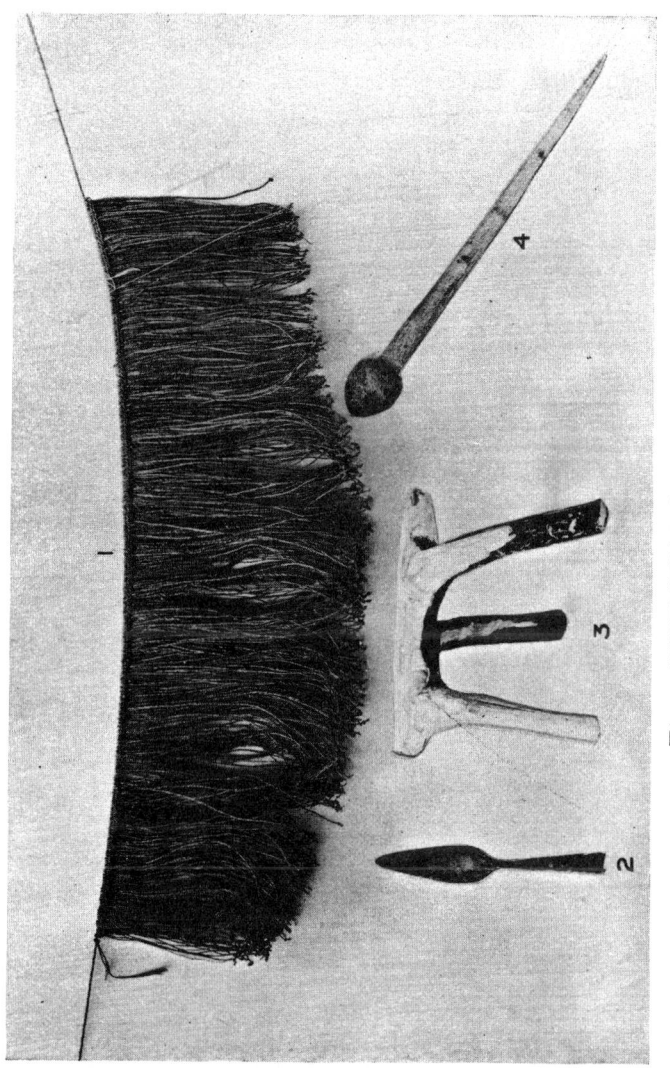

Fig. 4. ESSENTIAL ARTICLES

1. Short grass skirt. 2. Blade of spear. 3. Pillow (for men). 4. Club

Fig. 5. WOMEN'S GARB

1. Back section of married woman's two-piece suit. 2. Brass wristlet (many of these of graduated sizes may be worn). 3. Iron anklet (for girls). 4. Front section of married woman's two-piece suit. 5. Small coins, as tied on wrist. 6. Front section of married woman's dress (interchangeable with 4)

CUTTING THE TRIBAL MARKS 33

This rite changes the status of the boy from that of boy to man. Now he may attend all dances, he may carry a spear—in fact, all the privileges of a man are his. He also may exercise authority over boys who have not as yet had the tribal marks cut, and his sisters must treat him more respectfully than in the past, for now he has a voice in the affairs that concern them. However, he must render due deference to those who have had their tribal marks cut before him.

NUER CLASS NAMES

All the boys who have had their tribal marks cut during a certain period (usually consisting of from three to eight or ten years) are given a certain class name. While no Nuer knows his age exactly, he will always tell you to which class he belongs. Those who know the sequence of classes may judge his age approximately.

Classes of Nuer with approximate age now (1929).

Liereni	Tribal marks cut in 1927 (but only one authority for this name. All others call this class of 1927 Cai Yatni or Wum Kelunka).
Cai Yatni	Marks cut in 1925.
Lithgaac intot	Age now 20–25 years.
Lithgaac indit	25–27 years.
Carboc	27–35 years.
Dongonka	40– years.
Meker	50– years.
Bailoc	55–60 years.
Thut	60–70 years, but few living.
Nompiny	Probably none living now.
Cuatcuor	
Lajok	
Yilbith	

One cannot but admire the bravery and stoicism displayed by the boy, but it is a dreadful ordeal and a most gruesome sight. How long this custom will be continued is a question one cannot answer. Knowing the Nuer, one would be almost tempted to say that it will never be discontinued as long as there remains one Nuer boy unmarked. Yet one Christian boy showed definitely that he had not the same fear of the evil eye as his companions. But until the Nuer people as a whole become Christians, there seems to be but little hope that this dreadful practice will be discontinued.

Near Abwong the tribal marks are not cut as deeply as they are at Nasser, and heal much more quickly.

A mother who has borne six or seven sons may have these tribal marks cut on her forehead at the same time as her youngest son has his cut. It is considered a great honour.

One may occasionally see a woman who has from one to four cuts across her forehead, but that indicates that she has had severe eye trouble, and the cuts have been made to relieve that condition. The cuts are on the forehead only, and do not extend to the region above the ears.

At least one Nuer—a man—is an albino. His hair, unbleached, is flaxen. His skin is pink-white. I have heard that other members of the same family are albinos, although some of them are black, but I have seen but this one member of the family. His parents are black. Nuer have always been afraid of him, fearing that he has a god in him.

When he was old enough to have the tribal marks cut, no one wanted to cut them, for they feared this god that was supposed to be in him. But the boy was insistent, so finally he had the tribal marks cut, but they were not cut as deep as they usually are, and his scars are but very thin lines. He is not yet married. One wonders what a Nuer girl's thoughts will be as the sight of this man's cattle lures her father and brothers to give her to him.

Chapter Five

COURTSHIP AND MARRIAGE AND THE BABY

PREPARATION AND CHOICE

PROBABLY the most important event in the life of a Nuer girl is her courtship and marriage.

Her thoughts, even when a child, are upon her future husband, who he may be, what he may pay as the marriage price. Of course she often hears the village talk of how many cattle may be received for her. Sometimes her father or her brothers need cattle to help them out of financial difficulties incurred possibly through their own marriage plans. So they arrange the girl's marriage while she is yet a little girl and secure an initial payment of a cow or two in order to help them out. The husband does not take the girl to his village then but waits until she is older, and then he must pay the rest of the wedding price for her. Sometimes this man may be young, but more often he is an older man who has the cattle to help her father out of his extremity. And this older man may be planning to take her for his second or third wife, or possibly to get her for a wife for his son.

During her younger years she must have each ear pierced in from five to seven places along the outer edge, and she must have her upper lip pierced in the centre in order to wear a nail in it. When she is first taken to her husband's home white beads, as has already been noted, must be put in her ears, which will proclaim her status as a married woman to all who see her.

During her girlhood she must learn all the tasks that fall to woman's lot.

As she nears marriageable age she adorns her body with all the beads, anklets, wristlets, necklaces of various kinds, and rings that she can acquire. She also bleaches her hair and wears several headbands of beads.

Some neighbouring young man may be the cause of all of this effort on her part.

During the fishing season the lover is neither idle nor silent in his efforts to win the regard of his bride. He may be at the same fishing camp as she is; if so, he carefully grooms his best ox, then adorns his body with all possible ornaments and, getting some one to lead his ox, they circle around the camp. He dances as he follows the ox and sings praises of his ox, himself, and his sweetheart in loud tones that may be heard for some distance. This performance may be continued for some hours, especially the singing.

Usually the young man knows when he is not repulsive to the girl. When he has her assurance that she loves him, his people take up the subject of the marriage price with her people. The girl's physical appearance and possibility of bearing children figure largely in the estimate of her desirability. Also her temper and ability to control it are considered.

A certain day is agreed on for the marriage talk. Then all the men who are interested on the bridegroom's side assemble at the village of the bride-to-be. Places have been arranged for the relatives of the bridegroom to sit on one side of an open area, facing the relatives of the bride who are seated upon the opposite side.

A stick with both ends curved in a scroll design is carried by the speaker and twirled in the hands as he walks back and forth between the two factions and presents his arguments. He also wears a loin-cloth, often the skin of a wildcat. Sometimes it happens that each speaker is not the possessor of a loin-cloth, so a quick change is made, as one speaker concludes his speech and another prepares to take his turn.

One speaker at a time presents his arguments. If a relative of the bridegroom, he must try to get the girl for the least number of cows possible and still laud the girl as if she were worth many more cattle. The statements made by the bridegroom and his relatives are worthy of more praise than they usually get.

Each speaker carries the wedding stick as he talks, twirling it in his hands as he paces up and down between his hearers and waxes eloquent over his subject.

The relatives of the bride argue that such a fine girl as she should bring a maximum number of cattle, and they may specify which cattle they want if they know something of the cattle belonging to the bridegroom and his relatives.

The arguments continue and may even be resumed another day. Finally, if terms can be fixed that are agreeable to both parties, the argument is concluded (Fig. 10). But before the final decision, the bride is called and she states whether she agrees or disagrees with the decision arrived at. If she assents the bridegroom makes plans to collect his cattle and bring them, while the girl's people prepare for the wedding dance, for much food must be prepared as well as a good amount of the drink they make from dura.

But if the bride-to-be should disagree with the decision arrived at by her family and refuse to marry the man of their choice, her lot is not likely to be a happy one until they reach some sort of agreement (see Chapter VII.)

Possibly her brother is anxiously awaiting her marriage so that the cattle received may help him out in his own wedding plans. So he will not be inclined to listen to any objections from her which may mean the postponement of his own cherished plans. He may decide to discipline his sister by means of a good beating and may repeat it if the first dose does not bring the desired result in the form of her assent. Scolding is also resorted to, her lack of regard for her people being especially urged.

She may be strong enough in her determination to withstand the beating, but many girls succumb to the combined beatings and scoldings. She is then willing to send word to the groom that she assents to the family's arrangement for her future, but that assent does not imply that there is any willingness to be his wife or any love, but merely an assent to the marriage because of the persistent insistence of her family.

Sometimes, if the bride is very persistent in her objections, the bridegroom may withdraw his offer, not wanting a wife who will be so unhappy with him.

But if her objections are not too violent, the family usually depend upon scoldings and beatings to silence her, and the plans for taking her to her husband's village proceed. When she has gone to her husband's house, and if she is still persistent in her objections, he may beat her and his people may put thorny branches in front of the door, thus blockading her way of escape should she resist him. But they tell me that these cases are rare.

Many weddings take place in the dry season before the people go to the fishing camp.

If the girl has jilted the man who has paid cattle for her in order to take the man of her choice, as I describe in chapter VI, the wedding dance is not held, and there is no set time for giving her the garb of the married woman. She usually does not wear the beads in her ears that are the insignia of her married status. Keeping quiet and letting the commotion they have caused subside seems to be the object. Sometimes they have the wedding dance when the child is a year or two old, but it may be dispensed with entirely.

THE WEDDING

But if all has gone well the day is set for the wedding dance. The food is ready, word has been sent around that friends may come. The bridegroom and his people bring the cattle.

Girls in their grass skirts wearing every possible ornament are there. Men and boys, their bodies also ornamented as much as possible have come, carrying their spears and clubs, and some few with guns. From a distance the dance looks like a huge cloud of dust, but as one nears the scene the glint of spears is seen as the men run and jump up and down advancing upon some imaginary foe. The men dance in a mass formation, high jumping being a characteristic feature. The girls also dance in a group by themselves, led by the bride. They circle around the group of dancing men, but do not dance with them.

The bride leads the girls in the dance, facing them, which necessitates her dancing with her back to the mass of dancing men. One wonders how they manage to keep from being speared or from spearing some one in this crowd.

After the dance the feast is held, and then this part of the marriage ceremony is over.

Possibly the same night of the dance, but more likely several days later, the bridegroom asks that the bride be brought to his village. Her girl friends accompany her, timing their arrival so that it may be evening when they arrive at his village. They are attired in their dancing skirts.

A house is given the bridegroom for himself and bride; another house is given the girl guests who have accompanied the bride.

The bride gives her husband's family all her ornaments. She is not allowed to keep a single one of them.

The next morning before she comes out of the house where she has spent the night, the sister of the bridegroom or some other woman relative comes in to bring her the married woman's garb, which they have prepared for her, and such ornaments as they wish to give her. At this time the beads are put in her ears. When she comes out of the house she is attired as a married woman, and from this time on she must wear some kind of a loin-cloth.

Her girl friends and herself are guests at a big feast at the village of her husband that day, at which there is plenty of food and drink in evidence. When the feast is over, the girls return to the home of the bride's mother, for the Nuer bride does not stay with her husband but returns to her mother's home and spends most of her time there for the first year or two of her married life, although her husband may come to see her at any time, or she may go to his village whenever he wishes her to do so.

CUSTOMS CONCERNING MARRIAGE

A wife never eats with her husband nor sees him eat. And he, while he knows she eats her food each day, never sees any sign of it. This custom is usually observed for two or three years. Then they may eat together. The wife usually stays with her mother until her child is a year or two old at least.

The wife must render a daughter's allegiance to her mother-in-law, while her husband, in turn, must help his wife's mother as she desires, hoeing her field, or cutting her dura, or whatever she asks of him.

He never appears before his mother-in-law without a loin-cloth on, and for some time must never come to see her without sending word in advance.

The oldest son is allowed to be married first, and the family unite in getting his cattle ready for him. Then he

in turn helps the brother just younger than he, and so on
until all are supplied with the wherewithal to get married.

The oldest daughter in a family is likewise given in
marriage before her younger sisters.

Should a man have children by two wives, if one wife
dies, her son—even though he may be younger than
the sons of the other wife—may be allowed and helped
to get married before they do, the object being to supply
him with a housekeeper as speedily as possible. His half-
brothers are not supposed to be in as urgent need since
they have their mother to cook for them.

After a wife goes to live with her husband permanently,
if he suspects that she is paying attention to any other man,
he will probably beat her; or he may beat her for any
other reason if he so desires. He finds his spiked bracelet
specially useful at these times.

The greatest desire of a Nuer woman is for children.
She realizes that as long as she can bear her husband
children he will care for her. Should she fail him in this
her position is insecure, and he, no doubt, will try to get
another wife who will be able to give him his heart's desire.
The mother also realizes that her children will care for
her in her old age, even if her husband does take younger
wives, so her children make her position in old age secure.
The oldest daughter (when several years of age) goes to
live with her grandmother on her mother's side, providing
her mother is the oldest daughter of her grandmother,
or possibly this child may be the first grand-daughter.
So the grandmother is assured of help in her old age.

CHILDBIRTH AND AFTER

One frequently wonders how babies do manage to live in
Nuerland, when one considers how little care the mother
receives at the time of their birth.

She continues her work the same as usual before the baby's advent. Some neighbour woman who has helped other children into the world is probably on hand to help usher hers in. But the help given is negligible. They await nature's process, sometimes holding the mother up in a sitting posture with just her feet touching the ground. A sheep may be sacrificed to expedite matters.

When the child is born the cord is cut with a knife or a sharp piece of cane. It is not tied, and does not bleed.

The mother's food consists of gruel for some days. Then she resumes her usual diet. She cares for her baby, the neighbour woman or her mother bathing it for her for several weeks. She feeds the baby whenever it cries and usually gives it cow's milk until she has enough of her own for it.

When preparing the bath for the baby an earthen pot of water is heated. The baby is bathed in the late afternoon. The body is thoroughly greased all over, then the water (to us it seems like quite hot water) is splashed upon it, while the one who is bathing the baby rubs it briskly, massaging its back especially. Then when this part of the bath is over, she washes the child's eyes by licking them with her tongue, much as a cat would do with its kitten. The nose is also cleaned in like manner.

Various plans are resorted to in order to guard the baby from the evil eye. Charms are put upon its body, being fastened to necklace or wristlet. A rope is stretched out in the yard so that passers-by will know that strangers are not welcome.

The young mother sends word to her husband when she wants him to know about the birth of the child, so that he may come. No one asks whether it is a boy or a girl. The father may bring his wife a present of fish, and he may try to keep her supplied with fish for a little while.

THE CARE OF BABIES

A basket made of branches of a pliable wood is used as a baby-basket. A piece of animal skin which has had the hair scraped off, and is smooth, is put in the basket for the baby to lie on. If the mother has a piece of cloth she may cover the baby with it. Then a large woven grass mat is placed on top of the basket, being rolled up at each side until it just covers the top of the basket and keeps the sun off the baby and also keeps an active baby from sitting up in the basket while being carried. The mother always holds the side of the basket with one hand while carrying the baby in it upon her head.

When she arrives at her destination she carefully lowers the basket to the ground and unties the strings which hold the mat secure, and peeps at the baby. If it is asleep she unrolls the ends of the mat and lets them down to the ground at either side so that the baby may sleep undisturbed by light or sound. But if the baby is awake she carefully pulls the cloth or sheepskin covering that is over the upper part of her body round in front of her and over the baby-basket, and lifts up the baby under the cloth into her lap, so that no one—especially one with the evil eye—may see it.

A rattle is made by taking a small gourd which has a neck to it and putting a few pebbles in it. This is shaken vigorously when the child is crying.

A pacifier may be made for an older child (at least one year old or older) by taking the neck of a small gourd and cutting it off about one inch from the end. This may then be fastened to the wrist of the child with a string of beads and is ever ready when desired.

A little child is often given a strand of its mother's beads to play with, but its playthings are few.

The mother wears a leather belt with a border of shells;

she may call herself 'a woman who has just given birth to a child' for months afterwards, and try to solicit privileges on that account.

Nuer mothers love their babies and try to do all they can in their limited way for them. Whatever the child may lack, it does not lack its mother's love while she is living. But if the mother dies life is a different thing for the child that is left. A new-born baby demands food, and the artificial feeding of babies is an art entirely unknown to the Nuer. What to do with the small piece of humanity is a serious proposition.

Rumour says that they may bury the new-born baby with the dead mother, arguing that it will die soon anyhow, but I do not know of any authentic case where the live child has been buried. It is, however, very true that the motherless baby soon follows its mother. Five motherless infants have been brought to the mission at Nasser, as the people know that the art of the artificial feeding of infants is not unknown there. Two of these babies died, while three have lived so far.

TWINS

Twins are not uncommon, but are usually a cause of distress to their parents, for they are sure that one will die—and it usually does fail to survive. The mother always nurses one child at one breast and the second child at the other breast, and thus divides the supply of food as evenly as she can between them.

When a man is the father of twins, his brother will sacrifice a sheep before he eats with him so that no harm may come to the babies.

The Nuer has a superstition in regard to the burial of new-born twins. Rumour says that they prefer to tie the hands together and hang them up in a tree rather than bury them in the ground. I have never seen this done, nor have I known a case of new-born twins both dying.

I have heard in rather an indefinite way of triplets, but know of no authentic case.

One Nuer told me an almost unbelievable tale. I have tried to verify it from time to time, but have not been able to verify the main part of the story.

His story is as follows:—

A woman in a certain village gave birth to six babies at one time. She and her husband were much distressed as to what they should do to feed them. They finally decided that she could nurse two of them, but could devise no plan for feeding the others. So they decided to keep the two largest, healthiest-looking babies, and they took the other four babies, put them in a baby-basket together, and carried them to the forest which was about one and one-half miles away. They hung the basket up in a tree and left the four living babies—uncovered—in it. Then they returned to their village. The two babies they kept are well, strong children now, and are well cared for. My informant declares this to be true.

In my efforts to verify this tale I have found the name of the village, the name of the mother, the fact that they have 'twin' children the age that the two they kept should be, to be true as given by my informant. But I have not been able to verify his statement that she gave birth to six children.

Is the story a fabrication, or is it true and they are afraid to have it known to a white person? It is easy for a Nuer to say 'No' or 'I do not know', regardless of the facts, if he is afraid to give some information, or does not want to. They know that we would not approve of their method of solving their problem, although any one who knows the Nuer and his limited resources could easily realize what a serious problem the birth of six babies would be to them.

Chapter Six
DISEASE, DEATH AND BURIAL
DISEASES AND THEIR REMEDIES

PROBABLY the greatest cause of physical distress is the tropical disease which is commonly called yaws. It is prevalent throughout a large section of Nuerland, although it has not as yet invaded the Lau country.

This disease is characterized at the onset by aching in the muscles and joints, then lesions may form over various parts of the body. The mucous membrane of the mouth and nose becomes inflamed. Large ulcers may form on the limbs; when they do, the aching in muscles and joints usually stops. The bridge of the nose may be destroyed by inflammation.

Yaws is spread by contact with the discharges of the body of the person affected or discharges from the ulcers. It is not of syphilitic origin.

Sometimes the ulcers are quite large and deep; four to eight inches of tissue may be involved. Others, of course, are smaller.

The Nuer tries various treatments which have been recommended to him by his elders. Certain leaves may be tied around the neck, a massage with hot water may be given to relieve the aching muscles and joints. The ulcer may be scraped with a shell, the edge of the shell having been previously sharpened. If a kernel forms in the groin due to an ulcer on the leg, a special grass is tied around the ankle to relieve it. The disease may wear itself out in time without medical care.

The Government doctors have trained some natives to give the intravenous injections of the drug which is used to eradicate this disease. These native men usually accompany the District Commissioners on their rounds to collect taxes, and thus come across many cases of yaws. Probably few patients receive more than one injection, for the Government officials do not stay long in one place, but that at least does its bit towards the healing process and also towards the prevention of the spread of this disease. And no doubt this medical work brought right to the Nuer's door, helps to alleviate the pain caused by the loss of their cattle as they are taken for the payment of taxes.

During the rainy season when the Sobat river is navigable, and in all seasons on the Nile, the hospital boat—the *Lady Baker*—with at least one English physician and his helpers on board, provides treatment for all cases that can be reached in the towns along the rivers. Intravenous injections are given, and dressings are done. The dreadful ulcers receive one day's treatment at least. All who come to the hospital boat are treated for their various complaints. Those who wish may accompany the doctor to the hospital at Malakal, where they will receive free medical, surgical, and hospital care; they are given free transportation there and back to their villages again.

At Nasser there is a mission clinic. Here patients are encouraged to stay until they have received four of the intravenous injections and also a large daily dose of potassium iodide. Their sores are also dressed three times a week. Many, of course, leave before this course of treatment is completed, but others stay until a complete cure is effected. Skin grafts have been done at different times, three cases have been really successful.

Other remedies, such as bismuth, have been tried at this clinic, but beyond a palliative effect have been useless; the result has been time wasted for the Nuer and no definite cure. The intravenous injections were finally found satisfactory.

Fig. 6. Grass house

Fig. 7. A group in a Nuer village

Fig. 8. Tribal markings on forehead

Fig. 9. A carved gourd

DISEASE, DEATH AND BURIAL

It is surprising how quickly the ulcers respond to treatment at first. Later, when they are partly healed, the process seems to be slower, an ulcer may persist in being almost but not quite well for some time. Scar tissue breaks down easily, and the bare Nuer limb gets many a scratch and bruise which tend to cause a recurrence of the sore.

When a man is downcast because a sore is slow in healing, he may bind his hair closely to the head by sewing it with cotton thread until it has the effect of a hair-net. He may wear his hair like this until his cause of distress of mind and sorrow of heart is relieved. This in itself explains to those who see him that there is a reason why he is not adorning his body, and that he is not careless about his personal appearance without cause.

One attack of yaws does not render a man immune. Of course, those who have had no complete cure of the first attack are specially subject to a recurrence of this disease.

Leprosy is rare among the Nuer although neighbouring tribes are subject to it.

Trachoma probably causes more trouble in Nuerland than any other disease with the exception of yaws. It is so widespread, and is the cause of much partial and total loss of sight. Many have trichiasis, but when, as in the past, there was a doctor at Nasser many were relieved of this affliction by operation. At the Government hospital at Malakal, both in the past and in the present, relief was, and is, offered to all who come.

Flies are so numerous in this land that they have a very active part in the spread of disease.

Amoebic dysentery also takes its toll of life and weakens the people, although it is not as prevalent as some other diseases.

Pneumonia is hard to cope with in this land, and is much dreaded. As soon as the Nuer thinks that he has pneumonia he refuses to take medicine, asserting that if a victim of pneumonia takes medicine, the remedy will drive the disease all over the body instead of just letting it stay in the lungs. So the patient sits in the sunshine and the usual precautions are taken to guard him from those who might cast the evil eye upon him. Hot milk is given him to drink, if milk is obtainable. But he spends his nights shut up in a windowless house, the door being shut also, and possibly a small fire within for warmth. Many die, but some cases, even those who have had haemorrhages, have lived.

Sometimes when empyema follows pneumonia another Nuer will operate on the patient, opening up the pleural cavity in order to let the pus out. He may even cut the rib. The Nuer give you the name of the tree from which a twig may be cut in order to splice the rib. But I know of no one who has survived this operation. The patient is forcibly held down while this operation is in progress as they have no anaesthetics.

Various other diseases of more or less importance may be found. Cases of what they fear is a severe stomach disorder may eventually be found to be simply due to their fear of a curse.

The Nuer dread smallpox; when there is any danger of an epidemic of it they are quite anxious to be vaccinated. Smallpox is usually virulent in this country, and their dread of it is justified by the fact that it takes a heavy toll of life.

Chicken-pox, measles, and mumps may also be found. I have not known of any scarlet fever or diphtheria. Tuberculosis of the lungs is rare, although tubercular bone cases may be found.

Syphilis is not common, and when found its origin

DISEASE, DEATH AND BURIAL

may generally be traced to a source outside the Nuer. The Nuer have a superstition that dreadful things may happen—the nose may rot away, the head may split down the back—if they contract syphilis. Probably this superstition more than anything else tends to keep them from contracting the disease.

Gonorrhea, like syphilis, is not very common. It, too, may not infrequently be traced to a source which has no connection with the Nuer.

Children and the aged often suffer from malnutrition owing to their limited diet.

A Nuer child has the six central lower teeth removed when he is about six or eight years old. They frequently think that some illness the child has had is due to the teeth, and so have them extracted. Even though there be no illness the teeth are removed while the child is little. There is no such thing in Nuerland as painless extraction of teeth, judging from the cries we have heard and sore mouths we have seen.

Broken bones are also not infrequent, tiny splints for them are made out of cane stalk or some small twigs of a pliable wood. These are placed side by side and laced together, the splint thus formed being tied around the limb at the site of the broken bone.

Spear wounds are occasionally to be seen, but if they are the result of a fight, they are seldom brought to the clinic for medical treatment. The wound is cared for by the relatives of the injured person in the village so that the evil eye may not see the wound and retard its healing.

The art of the medicine man is often sought in order to cure any disease that baffles ordinary treatment. He (or she, as the case may be, for women are also adepts at this art) may remove (?) various things from the throat and stomach, and thereby relieve (?) the cause of distress.

They chant, they spit and blow upon the person. A sheep or an ox may be sacrificed. If the disease is persistent, more sacrifices are offered, more chanting is done. If successful in removing the cause of the disease, or even if the people are satisfied with what he has done, the medicine man usually receives a gift of a sheep or an ox for his services. But if the patient dies while under treatment the price paid is usually returned. The medicine men, or women, as the case may be, or those who are supposed to have a god in them, reap a good harvest in sheep and cattle from those who seek their services for relief from disease.

Medicine men usually wear the hair long and may wear a beard.

One common practice that is often resorted to for curative effect is bleeding. In case of a swelling or a bruise or muscular pain, many small cuts are made at the site of the pain in order to let the blood out and presumably the pain with it.

In cases of severe colds the chest is often cut in this way. When patients so treated go to the clinic for medical aid, it is often impossible to rub the chest with oils or apply poultices on account of the effect of such medicines on these little raw cuts.

Scorpions and snakes abound in Nuerland, and cause a great deal of suffering, but few die of snakebite.

The Nuer do not have much malaria. Occasionally one may see a few cases among them.

DEATH AND BURIAL

The Nuer are kind to their aged and usually respect their opinions, but death in Nuerland and the details of burial are gruesome. The climate of course necessitates quick burial, so as soon as life is extinct preparations must be made.

A description is given in Chapter VII of the way in which the body of a person who has been killed by lightning is disposed of.

For those who die of other causes a grave is dug. Relatives, usually the older ones, seem to consider it their right and privilege to dig the grave and bury the body. A twin does not help to dig a grave. The oldest child will break the ground at the site of the grave, but will do no digging if a parent is to be buried.

The work of digging the grave may last for several hours, for the ground is hard and the hoes used to dig with are quite inadequate. Sometimes relatives of the deceased, if near the mission, will borrow spades and hoes, and frequently welcome the assistance of a missionary in using them. If in a distant village they would simply follow Nuer customs as they are.

The grave may not be quite long enough, but the body is made to fit in. It is laid on the right side, so that the spirit may always walk aright and bring good to those left behind.

The body is stripped of all ornament and the head is shaved. To neglect this is to show disregard for the dead. Pieces of animal skin are placed under the right hip and ear and over the other hip and ear so as to protect them from the clods of earth.

Those who fill the grave sit with their backs to it, so that they may not see the earth fall upon the body of their dear one. Anybody who has once seen the Nuer burial can well understand why they should not want to see into the grave—it is a gruesome sight. After the burial those who have dug the grave bathe, and also wash the implements used for digging.

Only the family come to the burial. It is permissible to ask a few others, but it is seldom done.

The same day the stalk of the wild rice is swished all over the house and premises where the body lay after death, and is then put on the grave. The grave may be inside the house, or close to it outside. In the latter case it is plastered over with mud, and thorny branches are laid on it, or a cane-stalk fence is built round it, as the hungry hyena is ever near.

THE CLOSE OF THE MOURNING

After the burial the people eat little food for several days. Then some near friend comes and tells them that we all must die and urges them to cheer up.

The period of mourning varies. It may be from five to six months for a man and probably two months or more for a woman or child. A longer period of mourning is customary for a chief or his family.

When in mourning the hair is shaved off and it is not again cut or bleached until the period of mourning is over. No ornaments are worn. A rope is worn round the waist.

Word is sent to all the relatives that the period of mourning is to be finished upon a certain day. They come, sometimes from a long distance. The women pound dura and bring water.

A good friend of the family is master of the ceremony. This man brings lumps of earth to make a new fireplace. He makes a fire. He puts an earthen pot (a new one if possible) over the fire and puts dura mush on to cook. The women stir it.

The friend takes a spear in his left hand and a piece of grass in his right and walks up and down between the people and the food. He beseeches the god that this sorrow may pass. If the deceased is a woman or child, no spear is carried.

Sometimes this ceremony may be continued for hours. If the master of ceremony is tired another may relieve him for awhile. But when the ceremony is finished he dishes up the food himself. After all are served and have finished eating he cleans up the place, removing the fire and everything pertaining to it.

When all is clean he takes a clean half-gourd and sprinkles people, village, and houses with the water. The house of the dead person is sprinkled inside.

After this ceremony the ornaments may be resumed and the hair may be either cut or bleached. Now the mourners may attend dances again to which they have not been allowed to go during this period.

If the deceased has been murdered all the ornaments are not taken off and no rope is worn about the waist, but the rest of these customs are followed.

Chapter Seven

SOME NOTES ON RELIGION, SUPERSTITIONS, AND MORAL LAW

NUER GODS

THE Nuer has long feared and worshipped he knows not what. There are various gods, Deng, Wiu, Cwol, and others. Some have power over rain, some over crops, disease, death, or lightning.

Some animals are considered sacred, but what is sacred to one man is not necessarily held sacred by another. It may be the crocodile, or the land crocodile, or a certain kind of snake. Every Nuer is certain to have a sacred animal which he will neither kill nor eat.

Sheep and cattle are sacrificed on various grounds in order to appease one god or another.

When a person is struck by lightning and killed he is said to have been taken by the god of lightning—Cwol. His body is laid upon a rack that is made in his house or barn and then covered entirely—over, under, and on all sides—with wood, ash, and soil. The door of the house is closed and the house is left desolate except for its silent owner. A person who has been struck and killed by lightning is never buried in the ground as others are.

No one will touch a person who has been stunned by lightning until he regains consciousness, for fear the god in him may be transmitted by contact.

A Nuer always considers the relatives of one who has been killed by lightning as sacred.

Any one who has some physical or mental deformity may be considered as having a god in him and be regarded as sacred and avoided for that reason.

The Nuer worship is a worship of fear. The missionary feels as if he were living in Old Testament times, and

RELIGION, SUPERSTITIONS, AND MORAL LAW 57

in a way this is true. The Nuer find it hard to believe that God is a God of love. Even when they learn to love Him they still find it hard to trust Him when things go wrong. But the missionaries do not get too discouraged, for, after all, is not that habit world-wide?

A large portion of the Nuer tribe has never heard the Christian message. Of those who have heard it, few have yet made full response. Yet the influence of those who honour the name of Christ will make its mark upon the Nuer and lead to the forsaking of unworthy customs inherited from the past.

Although the Arab traders throughout Nuerland are Moslem, their religion has not appealed to the Nuer; the Moslem faith has so far gained no ground in Nuerland.

SUPERSTITIONS

The Nuer mind is full of superstitions, some of them being age-old. They believe them implicitly; 'Would our parents lie to us?' they ask when any doubt is expressed. Many of the superstitions have to do with cattle (see Chapter II) and marriage (see Chapter V).

A woman must never drink milk during her menstrual period. Nor at this time may she eat food which has been cooked in a kettle in which milk has been boiled. Why? Because to do so would harm the cattle.

If a woman is impregnated while still nursing a child, they cut a small piece off the ear of a dog and this is worn around the child's neck in order to keep it from harm. Any one walking in the footsteps of the father of this child may be the victim of dreadful things—his head may split right down the back.

If a child should have an attack of vomiting just after some strangers have been to the village, the strangers are at once suspected of having in part caused the attack.

Sometimes if the mission clinic is near they hurry there at once for relief. At other times the usual form of relief is sought—a sacrifice must be offered so that the child may not be further harmed by the errant stranger.

An anklet or wristlet made of large wooden beads of a certain kind of wood will protect from cuts from grass, but a man whose wife is pregnant may wear either anklet or wristlet made of red and white or black and white beads in order to accomplish the same purpose.

The Nuer fears a curse. Indeed, many a mysterious, inexplicable wasting away has been caused by this deep-rooted fear.

A bunch of a certain kind of grass standing up in the yard near the door will keep harm away from any sick person within.

The evil eye is much feared. There seems to be no definite idea as to who has this evil eye. Every one but one's own relatives must be suspected of it until one is sure that they do not possess it. The evil eye is supposed to harm whatever it sees, if it be a sick person, a sore, or even a new-born baby.

The disease becomes worse, the sore refuses to heal. All such misfortunes are attributed to the influence of the evil eye.

Patients who have ulcers to be dressed at the clinic are anxious that there be no onlookers when the sores are uncovered.

When a scar is healed but the scar tissue remains red, they plead piteously for a bandage so that they may keep it protected from the evil eye.

NUER LAW AND THE MORAL CODE

It is needless to say that Nuer law and their moral code are entirely different from that of our western world.

RELIGION, SUPERSTITIONS, AND MORAL LAW

They have a definite code, just as strict as any we may devise, but the emphasis is placed in entirely different places.

The Nuer does not live to himself. He is a member of his family, and his actions must be in accord with Nuer law as recognized by them. For should he trangress, he is sure to need their help.

Laws regarding sexual relations are decidedly lax according to our western standards. Many young men do not marry the mothers of their firstborn. Illicit relationship may exist between boys and girls. But when a girl reaches marriageable age she is usually under closer surveillance than before.

When a girl for whom part of the wedding price has been paid by a man whom she does not wish to marry, is dissatisfied with the arrangement made by her people because she cares for some more desirable and possibly younger man, there is only one way for her to cancel her engagement and thus free herself in order to marry the man of her choice. And this way is fraught with danger which may threaten for some time.

She will bear a child for the man she loves, and when her condition becomes known, her engagement to the man of her father's and brother's choice is automatically cancelled. Then for a time there is trouble. Her first lover wants his payment refunded at once. Her family want the marriage price from the man of her choice at once. Very probably he has not got it, so he takes the best way out of the situation (for him) and flees to some distant village, where he has friends or relatives, until the anger of the girl's people cools a little and they are more inclined to listen to him.

This is one of the times when he is thankful that he may depend upon his family and friends to help him out. They may or may not approve of his conduct, but they make the best of it now. When the family of the girl are willing to talk the matter over, representatives of her lover's family discuss the marriage payment with them and try to agree upon a suitable price. Usually some arrangement is made, and the man makes as large an initial payment as he possibly can, following it up by other payments as he is able.

Everything may go all right until the baby is born. If by any chance the mother should die and her death be considered as caused by the birth of the child, the father of the child is held to have caused her death. And serious trouble is on again between the two families. If a member of her family does not kill her lover, he is fined for her death.

But if she lives and the baby lives, all is peaceful and they may live the proverbial happy life ever after.

Likewise, a man may have a wife whom he has married, and one or more whom he has not paid for but who are his wives in reality and the mothers of his children. He keeps a house for each, and they are often good friends with his real wife, although they are never called his wives.

Thus a man may have children by his several wives, and it is quite common to ask children of the same father if they have the same or different mothers. Or one may ask children of the same mother if they have the same father, especially if their mother is an inherited wife.

When a man dies his wife is inherited by his brothers or other male relatives. In case they do not want her, she may be returned to her father's village and the cattle paid back.

Divorce is not unknown in Nuerland, but it is usually caused by the lack of children. If a wife cannot bear a child, or fails to bring living children into the world, the husband may demand the return of his cattle and return her to her father's village. Likewise, if the husband fails his wife in this respect, her people very probably will cancel the marriage and seek another husband for her. Representatives of both parties interested meet together and discuss the matter before the actual separation takes place.

One time, when asking a woman her name, I was surprised to hear her give a woman's name as her surname. Upon inquiry I found that she considered this woman whose name she bore as her nominal father.

The older woman was unable to bear children, but she had a number of cattle, so she paid for a girl who was considered as her wife. She got a man to come and live with the girl in order to beget a child. Then the child when born was considered as belonging to its mother and to her. She might give the man a cow, but he would have no claim upon the child or its mother then or at any other time.

This woman had several 'wives' and a number of children. She was the central figure of authority in her village and was considered a good leader of her people. I had heard of her before, but had never met her. She seemed to be a competent, capable woman, well respected by those who knew her and by the Government official as well. Her face, her speech and her manner were utterly different from what one might expect to find in one who—according to our western standards—had allowed herself to sink to depths of degradation.

Instead, one saw a Nuer woman a little past middle age, matronly, capable, and kind in appearance. She in in her way had sought children—and found them—and she loved them and cared for them.

Chapter Eight

CHARACTERISTICS, GAMES, AND MEASUREMENTS

THE REAL NUER

THE Nuer improves upon acquaintance. At first sight his better qualities are hidden from the casual glance and his body is anything but beautiful in its usual grey coating of cow-manure ashes. But to know the Nuer is to love him; for as one becomes acquainted with him he will begin to trust you, and you may penetrate the surface mask of reserve and find a depth of finer qualities within.

The favourite expression of a Nuer when asked a question which he does not care to answer is 'I do not know'. But as one becomes better acquainted with him he becomes willing to confide in any one whom he respects.

I have found refinement, consideration for others, courtesy, and faithfulness, as well as many other qualities, not only dormant but active in many Nuer.

The Nuer, probably because he has never been able to write, has a splendid memory, and is a good talker and imitator. He may relate some conversation he has heard and imitate each person in tone and manner. He can also imitate birds and animals.

SENSE OF COMMUNITY

When the Nuer eat they always use a common dish, and if one person is late to the meal, they await his arrival before beginning to eat so that all may share alike. Likewise, if one has had sufficient food and stops eating before the food is finished, the others ask him why he does not eat more before they proceed to finish their meal, eating the remainder of his portion of food.

We have had several small thefts of fruit at the mission, and Nuer living on the compound have assumed the part of self-appointed police without any idea of material gain for themselves. They have occasionally assumed such responsibility for the property of the white man as to make it necessary for them to declare a Nuer—even a relative—to be a wrongdoer.

A Nuer is faithful to his family and tribe, remembering his obligations to them and knowing that he may be sure of their support in times of urgent need. This pride in his tribe must not be undermined. Age-old customs and teaching have given him a heritage of which he may well be proud.

As the white man and the Arab mingle in his life and as western civilization touches Nuerland may the good in the Nuer remain undestroyed. May he not become dissatisfied because his ways are not those of western nations, but help to make his tribe better because he has lived in it. We must be careful not to designate as evil everything that is not part of our western civilization. If we teach the Nuer of Christ and they follow in His way, He will perfect their lives.

POISE

You cannot hurry a Nuer unless you can give their war cry—which brings immediate action.

Nuer have been taken to Khartoum, and while they were amazed at all the wonderful (to them) things which they saw, no one who saw them on the street could have guessed any of their thoughts by their actions. They were quiet and self-possessed amid surroundings that were entirely strange to them. One boy was even heard to remark that 'Khartoum had nothing to boast of, except that it did not have mosquitoes'.

64 CHARACTERISTICS, GAMES, AND MEASUREMENTS

I have seen a boy about sixteen years of age save a little girl from drowning. In less than a minute afterwards he was nonchalantly taking a bath, less concerned outwardly than if he had brought a fish out of the river instead of a human being.

The Nuer often asks for one thing or another, such as a safety pin, a piece of cloth or thread. Sometimes one is inclined to think that he wants something continually. But when one sees their meagre possessions one is surprised that they do not ask for more than they do.

FAITHFULNESS

One Nuer showed his faithfulness to his white friends in a way which caused him to give up his own cherished plans and take a long walk.

He had accompanied some of the missionaries in their launch to Malakal, a distance of about 200 miles. They were *en route* to Rejaf and were to board the Nile steamer at Malakal. He intended to buy some cattle and had been counting a great deal on this trip for several months.

As the Nile steamer left for the south at midnight a telegram was given to this Nuer and he was shown how to send it. The next morning he appeared at the post office with the telegram (post office and telegraph office are usually housed together in many places in the Southern Sudan). The postmaster—seeing the signature to the telegram—asked him if he was 'a person of the preacher's?' He replied 'Yes'; so the postmaster—a black man—asked him if he would take the post-bag to the mission. He thought of the cattle he wanted to buy, of this trip he had planned for so long, but he also thought of his white friends and of the eagerness with which they always welcomed the post-bag. So he immediately said 'Yes', he would take it. He gave his name to the postmaster, and

Fig. 10. The end of a wedding talk

Fig. 11. A Nuer woman and her baby

Fig. 12. The Nasser Mission on the Sobat

Fig. 13. The Nasser Mission (clinic in foreground)

CHARACTERISTICS, GAMES, AND MEASUREMENTS 65

received the heavy post-bag, for belated Christmas presents made it weigh more this time than usual.

The only thing that did not occur to him was that there might be any other preacher than the one at Nasser. He set out on his return trip to Nasser afoot, carrying a heavy bag of post—belonging to the Doleib Hill Mission which is about fifteen miles overland from Malakal, instead of to the Nasser Mission two hundred miles up river.

But he was blissfully ignorant of his mistake, and after a walk of seven days' duration, he delivered the Doleib Hill post-bag at the Nasser Mission, confident that there ought to be enough post in that heavy bag to gladden the hearts of all his white friends for some time.

He was deeply chagrined when told of his mistake. But possibly the memory of what he was willing to do for them will remain to gladden the hearts of his white friends longer than any news they might have received in that post-bag—had it been theirs.

Another Nuer, who knew how to steer the launch, showed his faithfulness to us by steering the launch all night when a hurried trip had to be made owing to illness. And later, even though Nuer are much averse to being close to dying persons, he would be found sitting on the porch outside the sickroom so that the nurse within— sitting by an unconscious, dying woman—might not feel so entirely alone. He had not been asked to stay there, he was not even expected to do so, but all he said was that he thought he would stay there so that the nurse might not feel entirely alone. It does not sound worth much—unless you are the nurse, alone with a hopeless case in the African stillness after midnight.

NUER GAMES

Boys make cattle out of mud, colouring them with ash or charred wood. They curve the horns and show quite a talent for clay modelling. They may also make clay figures of persons, and play with them and their cattle.

Possibly one of the principal games played with the clay cattle is that in which a mock wedding is enacted.

The boys make a number of cattle. Then one boy chooses the girl he wants. He and his friends tell her people that he wants to marry her, and they inquire as to how many cattle he is willing to give for her. The older people of the village may join in with the children in this —to them—delightful game.

The boy makes an armlet out of a gourd in lieu of the ivory armlet, he adorns his body with all the ornaments he can possibly get, borrowing from his friends in order to supplement his own meagre supply.

He and his friends meet with the relatives of the girl, and the wedding talk, which is a real debate, goes on. The bridegroom must try to get the bride for the least possible number of cattle without saying anything disparaging about her.

After the wedding talk, food may be served to the children and possibly they may stage a little wedding dance. This game lasts over several days, and the boy-groom gets a little experience to prepare him for the time when he will be required to bring real cattle and make a reality of what to-day is a game for children.

Interesting games are played with mud-balls.

Mud-balls are arranged four in a group and there are seven groups for each of the two players. One takes up two of the first group, the other player takes the remaining two, and so on, until the last group is reached when one player takes three balls while the other player takes but one. Then each player takes his balls in both hands, shaking his hands up and down vigorously and chanting 'bir chor' repeatedly. Then each player puts his balls down in groups of four each, and the player who picked up the one ball out of the last group finds that he has three in his last group now, while the other player who took three balls out of the last group is amazed to find that his last group now contains but one. They play it over and over again and enjoy it each time, but cannot explain it.

One boy was seen to do a trick quite cleverly by changing a mud-ball from one hand to another much to the amazement of his friends.

Another game is played with mud-balls in which points are scored as cattle with which to buy a wife. The Nuer enjoy this game very much, but they assure me it is far too difficult for me to learn and much beyond my feminine comprehension.

Boys make a ring of cane-leaves and then throw it, trying to throw a stick through it as it rolls.

They also play a game resembling shinny, and are quite clever at it.

Girls often play a game with pieces of cane-stalk about eight or ten inches long. One throws them on the ground and the way in which the different sticks fall indicates how many cattle will be paid as the marriage price; other points count as different things pertaining to the marriage. The pieces are thrown again and again, some positions in which they fall indicating the loss of a cow.

The girls play a game in which the hands are repeatedly clapped on the knees, and they chant a little song as they clap.

Little girls play house, pounding up clods of earth for dura, sifting it in order to get coarse particles out, and imitating their mothers in their work about the home.

On moonlight nights, the dance is a favourite amusement of both children and young people. A drum is made, possibly out of an old kerosene tin which has had the ends cut out and sheepskin pulled tightly over it, or it may be a large gourd with a sheepskin covering, or possibly it is made of a piece of the trunk of a tree, hollowed out and covered with sheepskin. But whatever its construction it emits enough sound to please any Nuer when it is beaten in the dance. The drummer beats a rather steady, rhythmic tune on it. One person usually chants a line of a song while all the other dancers chant an alternate line which serves as a chorus.

The dance is a group formation. Couples do not dance together.

The men run in in a long line and dance in a group. High jumping is a feature and one is amazed at the height they achieve. Quick advances upon an imaginary foe are made with much brandishing of spears.

One girl leads the group of girls, facing them and leading them as they advance and retreat before her. They keep time to the music with a quick movement of the head and hips.

A fiddle is made of a large piece of wood which has been hollowed out, or of a half-gourd, sheepskin being tightly laced over it. Strings are made of gut, and one can play as many as four different notes on some of the fiddles. While the player plays a tune on the strings of the fiddle he keeps up a steady, low accompaniment by thrumming the bowl of the fiddle with the fingers of the other hand.

Nuer are naturally musical, and many of them are quite good singers. They improvise many of their songs as occasion requires. Many of their songs pertain to marriage, many of them laud cattle or persons and proclaim their praises. Sometimes they voice their disapproval of some individual in song so that all may hear. They have a lullaby for babies also. Some of their songs are of a

CHARACTERISTICS, GAMES, AND MEASUREMENTS

vulgar type. In construction they are similar, consisting of a verse of one or more lines and a refrain. The verse is usually sung in a higher tone, the refrain being sung in lower tones. They seldom repeat any phrase over and over, but express the same meaning by the use of other words.

Another frequent form of amusement is the asking of riddles. If no one can guess the answer, the propounder of the riddle is asked if he or she would take so-and-so of the opposite sex as husband or wife, as the case may be. When an acceptable name is suggested, the propounder gives the answer to the riddle.

They have many riddles. Some seem anything but comprehensible to us, but they always tell us that 'a Nuer would understand'. Others are quite intelligible and good.

Sometimes Nuer children draw cattle or other animals; they always make the bodies rectangular in shape. A woman may draw on a gourd (Fig. 9) by making scratches and then rubbing them with charred wood, which gives the figures the effect of having been burnt in. The bodies of animals are drawn in rectangles, but other designs may be used. A border effect of points is often made.

MEASURING LENGTH AND HEIGHT

A Nuer indicates the length of small articles by extending the left arm and placing the tips of the fingers of his right hand at a point on the left arm. The distance between the tips of the fingers of the left hand and the place where the fingers of the right hand touch the left arm indicates the length that is meant.

When he desires to show the height of an animal he extends the right hand, palm downward. The distance between the ground and the extended palm is the height indicated.

When he wishes to show the height of a person the arm is extended, but this time the palm is held in an upright position, the distance between the palm and the ground being the height shown.

Distance is indicated by the number of hours or days required to make a journey between the two points mentioned.

Chapter Nine

WIDER RELATIONS AND INFLUENCES

THE NUER AS NEIGHBOURS

NUER living along the borders of Nuerland raid the neighbouring tribes and are raided by them, taking cattle. In the past they have taken people, but I do not believe that is done now to any large extent.

A number of Nuer have Dinka 'slaves' or servants, who have been taken in these raids, but they are usually treated as members of the family, except that the Nuer son or daughter takes precedence over the captive Dinka in being allowed to be married first. The Nuer name for Dinka means slave, and they consider them as an inferior tribe.

The Nuer sees nothing wrong in these border raids, but rather delights in the fact that it gives him a chance to show his prowess over his neighbour.

Sometimes one Nuer village raids another Nuer village, and this starts a feud that is hard to quell. It may last over several years. If some one is killed retaliation is sought. A life for a life is generally the rule.

Government interference is usually necessary to settle any large raid or incessant raiding.

Nuer wars and troubles between villages and different tribes are usually the result of cattle raids or the infringement of Nuer marriage customs.

In case two neighbouring villages are at war, especially if they be Nuer and Anuak, each assembles all their people and adherents. A war-dance and song are staged for the benefit of the opposite side, so that they may be impressed with the large number and possible prowess of their opponents.

THE NUER AND THE GOVERNMENT

The Nuer have occasionally had trouble which has required definite Government interference to settle it.

Several years ago the Government put on a patrol to quell an uprising in the Garjak section of Nuerland. There the Nuer saw his first aeroplane. To him it meant a huge boat that could fly and from which unseen guns could be fired. Hence they call the aeroplane the 'boat of the sky'.

The Nuer had great faith in one of their prophets, but when he failed to save them at this crucial time their faith in him was shattered. Again, more recently, they have been led astray by faith in another of their number—Gwek Ngundeng—and again they have found that he, too, was but a human being such as they, and no more powerful than any one of them would be.

Ngundeng, father of Gwek, had made a huge mound in the Lau section of Nuerland, and the Nuer considered this mound sacred. Many things were buried in it. But the mound was blown up by the English in the early part of their second patrol in order to shatter the Nuer faith in their god. The Nuer asked themselves—could this mound, a sacred place, be blown up? Was it possible? Then when they realized that it not only could be blown up, but had actually been destroyed, doubt entered their minds as to whether the mound had really been sacred or not.

When Ngundeng, father of Gwek, died, they then ascribed his power to his son Gwek. They had great faith in him, but when they heard that he had been killed in this patrol faith dropped to the zero point: 'Could a god be killed?' they asked. But if their faith in him died they still felt that he had been a most wonderful person, even if he were not a god. Shortly before word came of his death there had been a number of showers during the

WIDER RELATIONS AND INFLUENCES   73

dry season, and as this was unusual it had occasioned much comment among the Nuer. When they heard of his death a number of them at once assigned that fact as the cause of these rains.

In December 1927 there was a total eclipse of the moon which caused much alarm among the Nuer. They felt sure that it meant destruction to them and to their country, for was it not dripping blood? Later on, when the patrol was put on in part of Nuerland, they felt that it was just the fulfilment of what they had foreseen when the moon was in eclipse.

There is a saying among the Nuer that when they have plenty to eat they want to fight. That year, too, had seen a good harvest, and fight they did. There seemed to be many personal scores and old feuds that must be attended to that year, and then they declared it was all because the moon had predicted a year of trouble for them.

Not many Nuer have any conception of a country besides their own and the land occupied by a neighbouring tribe. They recognize their chief and his authority, but do not seem to realize their need of a larger, higher governing power.

Their acquaintance with this higher authority is limited. They see their cattle taken for taxes, they usually are willing to bring their difficulties to the District Commissioner to be settled; they are willing to be relieved of their physical ailments to some extent, and usually welcome the Government doctor and his trained assistants whom he sends out during the dry season.

The Nuer does not—or says he does not—see any good in paying taxes. Some of them feel that giving their cattle up for taxes is submitting without protest to a raid from a representative of another country, and they feel that if the Government can collect taxes (or raid their cattle as they call it), they certainly ought not to object when the Nuer raid the Dinka and take their cattle.

The Nuers learn to trust the District Commissioner and to respect his decisions, even though they be averse to their cause. They quite often prefer having him to settle a case rather than their Nuer chief. And yet one of the most respected and best loved of District Commissioners was killed by a Nuer recently.

In the spring of 1929 an epidemic of what was at first thought to be smallpox was reported in several villages. There were no fatalities, which is very unusual in Nuerland, for smallpox is very virulent and takes a heavy toll of life. The Nuer is accordingly much afraid of this disease. A clinic asked the doctor at Malakal to send vaccine, which he did, and many were vaccinated. The fact that the Government had sent vaccine for them and wanted to help them made a great impression upon the Nuer. Thus they realized that the Government did have something they needed and wanted to give it to them.

In time they may learn that they not only need what others can give them, but that they need to make their contribution to the world and to life outside of their own tribe.

There are not many guns among the Nuer. They depend upon the spear as their weapon, and it is usually not far from its owner's side. From boyhood on they are adepts at using the spear.

In the winter of 1928–9 the District Commissioner who was stationed at Nasser as his head-quarters had three aeroplanes come to Nasser. They stayed three days, their pilots being his guests. He wanted his Nuer to see aeroplanes at close range. He invited the people to take rides in them—the object being to show them that, while the aeroplane could be used for war purposes, it might also be used in times of peace. His interpreter was persuaded to take a little ride one day. Several chiefs were induced to try a ride, but one chief especially became quite frightened and a quick landing had to be made in order to keep him from jumping out.

The Nuer were quite alarmed when the planes appeared that morning, although they had been told some days before that planes were to come. Children ran screaming into the houses, men and women were badly frightened and dubious as to the purpose for which the 'boats of the sky' had come. Children stayed in the houses or near their homes, women would not go up to the merchants while the planes were flying.

Many were amazed by the short time taken for the flight from Malakal to Nasser, and realized to some extent that in case of need the planes with their guns might quickly come.

In the recent patrol the aeroplanes were again used as agents of war, so it is little wonder that to the Nuer the aeroplane is a thing of destruction, and they fear it accordingly.

The Government has shown an interest in the education of the Nuer and is eager to have schools among them. The authorities have sent several boys from Abwong to the mission school at Nasser and paid their expenses while there. These boys work in various capacities for the District Commissioner at Abwong, and when he is away he is anxious to have them in school. They were apt pupils. This same District Commissioner had one of the older boys from the Nasser school to conduct a school at Abwong for one season.

MISSION WORK AMONG THE NUER

The American Mission has long had a station at Nasser (Figs. 12 and 13). They work on evangelistic, medical, and educational lines. Itinerating work is also done by the members of the mission.

They have a church, clinic, and school, as well as three dwelling houses and a storeroom. A number of fruit trees have been planted and they have plenty of fruit for personal use.

The personnel of this station consists of from four to six adults.

Practically all the school pupils are working on the compound. They go to school for an hour or two at least and then work the remainder of the working day. Their wages are based upon their working hours, but all children, especially those who show any aptitude in learning, are required to attend school. Should they refuse, which they seldom do, they are dropped from the workers' list and some other eager applicant is taken on who is not averse to going to school.

At the Nasser Mission the work-bell rings at 6 a.m. All workers then attend the service with morning prayers and roll-call from 6 a.m. to 6.30. a.m. At 6.30 the workers go to their work and school opens. Lessons continue in the school until nine o'clock when chapel is held.

At 9.30 all workers are given one-half hour for breakfast. At ten o'clock the work-bell again rings and work on the compound and in the school is resumed until 1 p.m. when the working day is finished.

At 6.30 a.m. the clinic is opened by the Nuer helpers, the doctor (if there is one) or nurses not coming until 9 o'clock, except for supervisory or emergency work.

Arabic-speaking people are cared for at the clinic from 9–10 a.m. as are all the workers who come. From 10 to 10.30 a.m. the clinic service is held, which consists of songs, prayers, and a Bible story. All Nuer and Anuak patients, except those working on the compound, are supposed to be present if they wish for medicine that day; emergency cases are always treated at any time. After this service treatment is given to all who come.

On Sundays services are held in the church consisting of church service and Sunday school; in the afternoon a song service may be held. Or the song service may be omitted and a night church service held in one of the homes. The church can seldom be used at night on account of the ever-present mosquito. Sometimes the Bible lesson in church is given by a Nuer. Some of them show real talent for public speaking. There are from 150 to 160 Christians, but they are scattered throughout the various sections of Nuerland.

The church is not yet organized in the sense in which we understand organization. There is a committee of native Christians who have been appointed to supervise the receipt and expenditure of monies, but always with the aid of a missionary. A session is also appointed who help to examine candidates for baptism. Sometimes the examination they give is indeed rigid. The candidate's major sins of the past may be mentioned in detail. He is not merely asked to forsake sin, but those sins to which he is more subject are mentioned in particular. Sometimes a member of the session may be suspended, owing to some sin in which he has actively taken part.

Sometimes it seems as if the results of our work were small. Then some incident fills us with encouragement and we are amazed to find the extent to which the Nuer Christians are willing to trust Him whom they have so recently accepted as their God.

School work is carried on five days a week. The fact that all books must either be written in this language or translated into it is a serious handicap, for this translation work takes time, and it is hard to keep new material prepared for the higher classes. English is taught to some extent, but the Nuer is taught in his own language first that he may learn to appreciate the things that are Nuer.

Student teachers are employed, pupils being thus trained to teach those who have not as yet learned as much as they have. In this way, a pupil teacher, returning to his village, knows how to teach what he has learned, be it much or little, to others.

A Nuer who is also a pupil in the advanced classes is supervisor of the school under the direction of a missionary.

The pupils do not pay for tuition. Only one case is known where a pupil at this school paid for his schooling in any way. This man was only able to go to school for an hour a day, but he was anxious to keep up with his class who were having two hours' instruction daily. He paid a Nuer for his services as private tutor each afternoon. This aspirant after an education was an Anuak, both he and his tutor were pupils in this school.

The Nuer boys sent by the Government official at Abwong to this school formed the greater portion of a boys' boarding school while they were there. The two men who are working for the District Commissioner at Nasser as his interpreters attend school all the time when they are not on trek.

The mission is busy now getting the books translated which were recommended by the Rejaf Language Conference of 1928.

There is a Roman Catholic Mission in another section of Nuerland, but I am unable at this time to give any definite facts about the work. I understand that one of the main features of it is the school. This mission will also use the course of study recommended by the Rejaf Language Conference.

Missionaries usually are victims of the ever-prevalent malaria but it does not daunt them, and they continue to love their people and their work.

But much remains undone; there is urgent need of mission work along any or all of the present lines—evangelistic, educational, and medical.

Chapter Ten
THE NUER LANGUAGE
RESULTS OF STUDY

THE Nuer language in most points has some similarity to the other Nilotic languages, having many of the same sounds, but it is a distinct language in itself, and not an outgrowth of the others. Possibly it shows more similarity to the Dinka than to any other of the neighbouring tongues.

Various systems have been used in reducing this language to writing, but no one system has been found which seemed to satisfy the different missions and the Government officials who were using a Nilotic language. So in April 1928 the Sudan Government called a conference at Rejaf, where representatives of the missions and governments engaged in work among the Nilotic tribes were present.

The Government had invited Professor Westermann of the International Institute of African Languages and Cultures to prepare a system of certain signs to represent the unusual sounds of the Nilotic tongues. Professor Westermann was present and the new system was tested with the various natives at the conference who were present for that purpose from the different tribes.

Thus for the first time a common system was adopted for general use throughout all the Nilotic tribes wherever any effort is being made to reduce any of these languages to writing. This in itself is a big accomplishment, as all missions as well as all Government officials have accepted the system.

A standard course of study for the elementary schools was also adopted.

The Nuer language so far has not been very largely

THE NUER LANGUAGE

transmitted to paper. The two missions working among the Nuer have a limited number of school-books printed in this language. The American Mission has six readers, one of which contains much folk-lore. They also have a translation of Dr. Mary Blacklock's book on Hygiene. But the white man when he arrives in Nuerland has but little to help him to a quick understanding of the language. A Nuer-English dictionary has just been published, and an English-Nuer dictionary will soon be ready for the publisher. In each a few pages of Nuér grammar has been included. But so far the white man has had to extract his knowledge of the language from the Nuer himself, and this process takes time—and patience.

The Nuer language as I have found it has an extensive vocabulary. I have listed over 3,100 words in the above mentioned dictionary, many of them root-forms only, and I constantly find how limited my knowledge of the language is. One finds new words each day. It seems like an endless mine.

In working on this language distinctive points are noted. The same forms are used for all genders in pronouns. A change of vowel or an additional vowel is common in forming the possessive of a noun. Many proper names are the same in both masculine and feminine cases, but the prefix *nya-* or *nyan-* is always used with the feminine. The supply of adverbs seems inadequate, but possibly we have not discovered them all. Also the names of many virtues are lacking, and we frequently find that we need more adjectives. Change of inflection plays an important part in this language in making negative forms and plurals.

Nuer sentences are short. The Nuer seems to prefer a new sentence instead of using many connectives. He often states a fact, modifying it in the next sentence, e.g. 'Every one went away, I only was left.'

The Nuer language has a wealth of animal and bird stories, tales of the origin of the tribe and folk-lore. Also games, songs, riddles, and superstitions. All of these are as yet practically untouched by the pen. A sort of cannibal-ogre combination, capable of changing into an animal, is usually a prominent character in their folk-lore.

The language contains no word for 'thank you' as far as I have delved into it, but one does not need to be in Nuerland long to discover that the Nuer has a word for 'I am mistaken', and is willing to use it.

TIME, SEASONS, MOON, AND STARS.

The Nuer gauges time by moons, the light or dark of the moon. He knows the stars, and has names for many of the constellations. He is a keen observer of them and makes his own observations concerning them. Orion's belt is called 'gat rum juk'. One star is supposed to be a man leading a horse, the second star is supposed to be the horse, while the third star is another man driving the horse as he follows him.

The evening star is called 'Lipai chiing', as it is considered to be like a girl in the village waiting for the moon to come up and when it does come up, she goes away with it. Hence the name, which means 'wait in the village for the moon'.

The Southern Cross, the Little Dipper and other constellations are also noted and named.

The Nuer firmly believes, as already noted, that the cattle see the new moon the night before it is visible to the human eye. I have frequently asked them concerning this. The date upon which the cattle see the new moon always seems to be the date specified upon the calendar as the date when the new moon should be visible. Yet the Nuer has no calendar.

THE NUER LANGUAGE 83

The year is divided into months according to the moon. There are four seasons. The fishing season usually starts in the latter part of December or the first of January. It lasts probably three months, then when the rainy season starts and the river rises, the spring season begins. The spring season is called 'rwil' while the fishing season is called 'mei', or as we would pronounce it 'mae'. The season in which the dura is growing is called 'tot' (pronounced 'tawt') and corresponds to our summer season. The autumn season is called the season of winds or 'jom'.

There is no Government thermometer at Nasser, and I can give no definite scale of temperature. I have had a thermometer in my sitting-room for several years—(a room with brick walls and grass roof, two large windows and two doors). The minimum temperature which I have happened to note was 56 degrees F. The maximum in this room was 105 degrees F. As a rule the temperature ranged from 84–100 degrees F. Of course different temperatures may be registered when the thermometer is placed elsewhere. I just give the temperature of the room where I was working during the hottest part of the day. Others have found their thermometers to register 110 degrees.

However the sun does a thorough job in heating the bath water. The pipes are on the surface of the ground and the water is often far too hot to use until after it has stood for a while, as there is no cold water to cool it with.

The day is also divided, so while the Nuer cannot tell what time it is by giving the hour, they can give a very definite idea of what they mean.

au e durdur	not yet daybreak.
ci au bak	daybreak.
ci caŋ kany	sunrise.
thal caŋ	about ten o'clock.

caŋdar noon.
buoka caŋ middle of afternoon.
ke thiaŋ late afternoon.
ci war lip early evening.
war night.
wardar midnight.

('ci' is pronounced 'chi', 'caŋ,' is pronounced 'chang', 'thiaŋ', is pronounced 'thiang'.)

NAMES OF NUER—DETERMINING DATES

A Nuer has a splendid memory, but dates, birthdays, and anniversaries are not the things he stores away in it.

A parent may tell you in what season of the year a child was born, but after a few years the number of its years becomes but a confused memory.

When some special event has transpired which fixes a date firmly in their minds, they may date an event from that time. The time when the English patrol was in the Garjak country is often used when dates are discussed; an event may be dated either so long before or after the 'boats of the air' came. A flood, a famine, a year when wild animals were numerous, all may be used to mark time.

When the age of a child is asked it may be determined from the reply to such questions as:

does he crawl? one year.
is he weaned? (if so) three years old.
does he herd sheep? 8–12 years old.

For later ages one may ask 'when will he have the tribal marks cut?' (tribal marks are usually cut when the boy is from 14–16 years old). After the tribal marks are cut, age may be determined by the class name, providing the sequence of classes is known (see Chapter IV.)

A woman may be asked 'If you were a man, what class would you be in?' and her age determined by the answer.

A child is often named to commemorate some event that has just occurred so the name in itself gives an idea of the date: for instance 'Rath' is famine. Possibly the boy was born in a famine year. If the family are in mourning when the child is born, it may be called 'Mun' if a boy or 'Nyamwon', if a girl. The name means 'ground' or 'daughter of the ground'.

An orphan—whose mother is dead, although the father may still be living—is often called 'Ret' which means 'orphan'. 'Bany Piny' is also a name given to an orphan which means 'left on the ground'. A girl orphan is often called 'Nyaret'.

Twins are often given names which mean 'the leader' and 'the one who was left', indicating their order of birth. The feminine prefix is used if a girl.

Buth	the leader (a boy).
Nyadwoth	the one who was left (a girl).

A child always takes the personal name of its father as its surname, although in so doing the possessive form of the father's name is often used, but not always.

Mun Dup	name of father.
Rath	personal name of son.
Rath Mwon	full name of son.
Pec Kak	name of father.
Nyalira	personal name of daughter.
Nyalira Pec	full name of daughter.

A girl's name almost always has the prefix 'nya-' or 'nyan-' meaning 'daughter of'.

A girl retains her father's personal name as her surname throughout life as she does not assume her husband's name when she marries.

NUER GREETINGS

The Nuer have a number of forms of greeting and are rather strict in observing their usage.

Probably the most common form is 'chi nienu', or 'have you slept well?' To this greeting, one responds with a grunt resembling an 'aw' sound. Then the second greeting is given. In response to this you again reply with a grunted 'aw'. Then you, in turn, ask your friend if he slept well, and he responds with the grunted 'aw'; you give the second greeting and he responds in like manner.

Two greetings are always given; the first one is always 'chi nienu', but the second one may vary; as—

    chi palu   have you prayed?
    chi tolu   have you smoke (in your village
                  —the inference being that you
                  have a fire and are cooking food)?
    malu   are you well?

Any one of these three may be used as the secondary greeting.

When two people meet and have perhaps discussed some matter before greeting each other, they will use this first greeting before they part as well as the one used when leaving.

In parting, the one who is leaving says 'ku lo nien a gwaa' which practically means 'may you be well after I leave'; to this the responsive 'aw' is given. Those who are left behind reply with 'wir a gwaa' meaning approximately 'go in peace' which draws the responsive 'aw' again.

It is not a Nuer custom to shake hands with a person. The Nuer greeting is given by word of mouth. Nuer who shake hands with one are imitating their Arab or white brothers.

When a guest comes to a village he sits down. His host or hostess may place a sheepskin on the ground for him to sit on. He sits there, and presently his host and hostess greet him.

'Gwadin' and 'madin' are titles of respect given to men and women respectively when a younger person addresses an older one. An old woman, wishing to use a term of respect toward a young man may address him as 'wadin'.

A younger man may greet an older woman by taking her hands in his, spitting upon them and rubbing them. Then he bends his head and she spits on the top of his head. Or he may take her hands and blow upon them, and then incline his head while she spits upon it.

A father, returning from a journey, usually spits upon the heads of his children.

Girls who are nearing the marriageable age begin to use this method of greeting one another if they have not seen each other for some time; each in turn inclines the head while the other spits upon it.

In explanation of this method of greeting it might be said that the Nuer method of spitting when greeting any one is different from his method at other times. At the time of greeting he really sprays the head or hands, as the case may be, with a very fine spray of saliva.

Chapter Eleven

NUER FOLK-LORE

THE Nuer language is rich in folk-lore. Many tales have been handed down from one generation to another. In these tales the people implicitly believe.

Nuer folk-lore may be classed under four different headings. There are tales which relate to the origin and history of the Nuer tribe; some of these have already been given in the text. There are animal and bird stories. There are tales whose central figure is a sort of ogre; these correspond in part to our own fairy tales. There are also riddles, some of them handed down from generation to generation. Several specimens of animal, bird and ogre stories and a few of the Nuer riddles are given here. On some future occasion it may be possible to print a fuller collection, with the Nuer text.

Acknowledgements are due to Mrs. P. J. Smith of the American Mission at Nasser, who has been instrumental in getting the Nuer interested in writing their folk-lore for use in the schools, and to Nyan Yut, who wrote down the riddles for me as 'a present to my sister'.

THE COMING OF FIRE

Long ago there was no fire in this place. When men wanted food the grains of dura were pounded one by one until the place in which it was pounded was full. Then the pounded dura was ground, wetted, and put to dry in the sun. When the top dried it was picked off and eaten. What remained dried again after a time and was again picked off and eaten until all the dura was finished.

One day Dog set off on his travels to hunt for fire. He arrived at the village of a snake who was cooking food. When he appeared they said 'Make way for the traveller' and moved aside. He sat down by the fire. Suddenly he wrapped his tail round a burning stick and ran away with it swiftly. Snake raced after him, but could not overtake him. He brought the burning stick back with him and gave it to the people saying, 'Blow the fire'.

The people soon cooked their food with fire.

THE STORY OF KIIR

Yul is he who gathered Kiir up in the river.

Yul and his people were travelling when a gourd fell from the heavens with a spear and the skin of an animal. The gourd was very big, higher than the people. Yul said to the people 'You take the gourd.' Everybody feared because the gourd was so big. Yul was not afraid at all. The people who travelled with Yul fled, so he was left alone beside the gourd. He split it open himself, and Kiir came out of it. One side of the gourd had seeds.

Kiir is a sorcerer. Yul said to him, 'We are going to the village.' When Kiir refused to go Yul left him. Kiir is a bad sorcerer and went off alone. When he saw elephants and other animals he would pierce their hearts.

One day the people came to Kiir and besought him. 'Let us go together to the village. We will give you a girl.' At first Kiir would not go, but when the people wearied him with their talk he went. In the village they gave him a girl and he begat children.

Kiir has a family now.

LEST THE EARTH SHOULD QUAKE

Long ago people walked slowly lest quick walking should cause the ground to quake. They kept on doing this. One day a man raced by at great speed. 'You will cause the earth to quake,' they said. But he took no notice of what they said. When the people saw that the earth did not quake under his footsteps they walked fast too. The earth did not quake at all.

THE WORDS OF GOD AND OF THE PEOPLE

Long ago God and the people talked together. God asked if they would rather live for ever, or die. The people told God that the earth was growing full of people; it would be better that some should die and make room for those who come after them. God said, 'Oh! All right!'

That day Dog went among the cattle. When he had seen them he went to the village. He cried, 'Did God talk to the people to-day?' They answered 'The people and God talked.'

Dog asked, 'What did he say?' The people replied, 'He told us to choose life or death. The people chose that some might die while others came after them.'

Dog said, 'What did he do?' The people said, 'He threw a stone into the river'. Dog said, 'You show me the place.' They showed him the place. He dived. He brought up a little stone. People are always restored by it.

THE WORDS OF A MAN

A man found snakes fighting one day. As he came near and looked at them he saw that one snake had been killed. He reproved them. He said 'Go away.' The snake gave him a charm saying, 'By means of that charm you will hear all things. When the rat talks, you will hear it. When the cow talks, you will hear it. You will hear everything that is said.' The man passed on. He came to the village.

At night the man's wife locked the house so that there was no open place. All was quite dark. She and her husband lay down to sleep. A mosquito came to the door. It examined the house. It found no way in. The mosquito exclaimed, 'They have locked the house very tightly. How can one get in?' The man understood and laughed. 'What are you laughing about?' asked his wife. 'Nothing,' said he.

Again, a rat came. He examined the door. He found it fast closed and left it. He tried the eaves of the house and got in. He searched everywhere. He wanted butter. He found none. He said, 'Oh, where has that woman stored her butter?' The man laughed. His wife asked him, 'What are you laughing about?' He answered, 'Nothing.'

In the morning the man went to his barn. He let the cattle out. When it was nearly milking time his wife came to milk. When she arrived the cow said, 'Of course you come, but you will not milk me to-day. I will withhold my milk. My calf will drink it afterwards.' The man laughed. His wife asked him, 'What are you laughing at?' He answered, 'Nothing.'

The wife left the cow. She returned to the village. Then the calf sucked its mother.

Next day the wife again came to milk. The cow again withheld its milk. In the afternoon the woman's child was ill for want of milk. She brought it to the barn. She talked to her husband. She said, 'That calf will kill my daughter.' The cow interrupted, 'What! My daughter will kill your daughter?' The man laughed. His wife asked him, 'What are you laughing about?' He answered, 'Nothing.'

When it was nearly sunset his wife said, 'I will get a divorce.' She called all the people. They came to her husband's place. They seated themselves. They said to the wife, 'You and your husband talk. We will listen.' The wife talked. She said to the people, 'When we lie down to sleep, my husband always laughs at me without any reason. When I ask him why he does it he hides the reason from me. That is why I object to him.'

Then they asked the husband, 'Why do you laugh at your wife? Tell us.' He answered, 'Nothing.' They said again, 'Tell us.' He answered, 'Men, if I tell it, I will die.' They said, 'Tell it, man! Do not hide it.' He replied, 'Oh, men, I will not tell. I will surely die.' They urged him. When he was worn out he told them. He said to the people, 'This is the reason why I laughed when we were lying down in the house. After a while at night the mosquito would talk. It would say, 'Who is this woman that has locked up her house so tightly? Where can one get in?' 'That is why I laughed.'

The man died, as he had said. The people cried. Some of them dug a grave. As they were about to bury the body a certain snake hastened to the desolate spot. It wrapped itself round the body. It stuck its tail in the nose of the dead man. He sneezed. The people were amazed. Some of them said, 'Is it his god?' Others replied, 'Why ask who it is?' When the man stood up the snake left.

When the man had quite recovered he travelled through the desolate places. He found the snake under a tree. The snake said, 'But why did you tell? Long ago when I gave you that charm I told you it would make you hear all things.' The man replied, 'They urged me, so I told them.' The snake said, 'Oh!' Then the snake gave him another charm saying, 'You will hear the words of the birds which eat the kaffir corn. When a bird eats the kaffir corn in the field you will hear.'

The snake went away.

The man returned to the village. He heard many things. When a bird was eating the kaffir corn, if another bird came near the first one would say, 'Bird! Do not come. We will be seen. I am eating quietly. This is my place. Let us separate. The field is large.' After a while another bird would reply, 'What! I shall be found out.' A third would break in, 'How will you get out? Perhaps they will find us.' 'Let him go' cried one bird. 'I am not going,' said the other. The man laughed there in the kaffir corn.

When the birds had finished talking he urged them to go. They scattered. The birds were provoked because one bird said to him, 'If you had not come they would not have found me.'

The man always held that snake sacred as his god.

THE STORY OF THE YOUNG WIFE

There is a story of a man who married and took his wife to his village. His work was to go out and herd cattle. One day at the edge of the swamp he found an ogre who was dying of hunger. The man had caught an antelope. He beckoned to the ogre, though he knew what he was. He showed him the antelope. The ogre ate of it. Then he drank water. When he had finished drinking he asked the man, 'Did you know who I was a little while ago?' The man replied, 'I knew you were an ogre.' The ogre said, 'Oh! You saw a person that was starved.' I was helping a person,' said the man. The ogre replied, 'Oh! I have nothing much to say, but I will show you something.'

He dug up a sweet potato and gave it to the man. The man asked, 'Is there no other?' The ogre gave him one. He ate it. Again he asked the ogre, 'Is there none left?' He was given another. He asked the ogre, 'What is this called?' The ogre replied, 'It is called—what?' He signed to the man with his head. He said, 'This belongs to you alone. Do not show it to the people.' The man went on digging his potatoes.

When he brought the cattle back to the village his wife gave him mush. He refused it and called some one in to eat it. The next day he went out with the cattle again. He dug up his sweet potatoes again and ate them. He had plenty. When he brought back the cattle his wife brought him mush. He refused it. Every day it was the same.

One day his young wife said, 'People of my village, why does my husband always refuse my food? Why does a man want to marry a wife?' The people replied, 'A man marries in order to have some one to cook his food.' The wife said, 'Now my husband always refuses my food.' The men who were of the same age as her husband said, 'We do not know what he is doing.' They said, 'Tell us,' but he said nothing. They left him there.

Next day the man took the cattle out. His wife followed him. He dug up his potatoes and came to the edge of the swamp to wash his hands. His wife arrived. 'Oh, yes, that is why he always refuses my food. Yet he married me by paying cattle for me. Oh, but your mind is lost.' The wife left. The man was taken aback. He ate what he had dug up. He brought the cattle back to the village.

Next day when he brought the cattle out he hunted for his sweet potatoes, but he could not find them. In the afternoon he went home. He was offered food and ate it. He did not refuse mush again.

THE MAN AND THE CROCODILE

Long ago a man went to the river's edge to get a drink of water. As he put his mouth to the river to drink a crocodile caught him and brought him to its house in the bottom of the river. This house was dry. There was no water in it. The crocodile brought the man in.

The man stayed there. It was not possible for him to

get away for the dooryard was full of small fish. When he tried to get out the small fish cried. The crocodile on hearing them hurried from wherever he was. The man seeing the crocodile coming would fall to the ground and look forlorn.

One day the crocodile went off to a distant place. The man, taking courage, sprang out of the house. At first he was under the water. When he came to the surface he breathed a very big breath. He gasped a big gasp also. He floated on the top of the water. He reached the land. He sat down for a little.

When he was rested he stood up. He started out. He journeyed. But he did not know that wells had been dug ahead of him. The tops of the wells were covered. They looked like the rest of the ground. As the man went on he fell into a well.

And an elephant came and fell into the well also. It stuck fast in the middle of the well. It did not reach the bottom. The person was in the bottom of the well. The elephant was in the upper part. At first the elephant filled the mouth of the well. There was no open place. Then the man found a small place at the side of the elephant. He put his nose to it. His breath came. So he did not die.

The people, hearing the cry of the elephant in the middle of the village, ran. They arrived. They jumped in, cutting off pieces of the elephant. They cut the whole elephant up. The man was all the time in the bottom of the well. His body was very red from all the blood. When the people had finished skinning the elephant he called to them, 'Children! Oh, men! Take hold of my hand.' The people refused. They said, 'Is it not an ogre?' They left.

One man returned. He said, 'If it is a person I will go and find him.' He came to the top of the well. He asked,

'Are you a person in the bottom of the well or are you an animal?' 'I am a person,' was the reply. The man knew from the voice that a person was speaking. He went to the bottom of the well. He brought the person out. He took him to the river. He was bathed. The man took him to his own place and massaged him with hot water.

The person's body was soon well. He never went away to any other place. He belonged to the man who brought him out of the well.

THE CROCODILE AND THE WHITE FISH

Long ago the crocodile lived in fear of a certain fish. He went some distance away but he and the fish met again. Crocodile passed by at the side. Fish said, 'You are always afraid of me.' Then he added 'Come near to me; see my mouth.'

Crocodile refused because he was afraid. 'You are a big person, Fish, they often tell me you will eat me. That is why I am afraid.'

Fish said, 'Do not fear; I have no teeth.'

'Open your mouth' said Crocodile 'and I will see from a distance.'

Fish opened his mouth. Crocodile looked in. He came close by. He saw no teeth. He said to Fish 'Heretofore I have feared without cause.'

They travelled for a little together. Then Crocodile ate Fish.

THE ARGUMENT OF THE FROG AND THE OSTRICH

One day the ostrich had an argument with the frog. The frog said to the ostrich, 'Boy, they always brag about your running. But if you and I ran a race, do you think you could then keep my body in sight?' The ostrich replied, 'Why, man, could you pass me?' After their argument the frog said to the ostrich, 'I will name the day for the race. We will choose a rainy day when the water lies in puddles on the ground.'

They waited seven days. Then when it had rained all the frogs assembled themselves together. They lined up for a long distance. They had all made a plan. The frog went to notify the ostrich that he was ready.

They raced. After a while the ostrich said, 'Am I not beating the frog?' But the frog who was waiting for him at that place exclaimed, 'Tawt! You cannot beat me.'

The ostrich set off to race again. Again he called to the frog, 'Am I not beating you now?' But the frog who was just ahead exclaimed, 'Tawt! You cannot beat me, man.' This went on until the ostrich was worn out. He was so exhausted that he died.

None would have beaten the ostrich if a plan had not been laid against him.

THE STORY OF THE MONKEYS

God made the monkey somewhat like a person.

They say there are many monkeys in the Garjak country. When the people come to the river the monkeys also assemble there. They sit on the opposite side of the river and they play. Then half of them will go to drink while the others throw clods into the river. When they have finished the others drink while the first lot throw clods. Then the mothers come guarding their children. One will put her child on the ground, dip up water with her hand and give it to her child. After the little monkeys have drunk the mothers drink too.

The young monkeys pull the tall grass. They spend the day chewing it. In the afternoon they come to their village bringing their mothers tall grass. The monkeys go fishing too. They kill very small black fish.

Then the young ones sit on the river-bank or gather wood while the male monkeys sit down.

The people come to watch the monkeys as they eat. The big person will divide the fish among them all, giving himself some. They will eat. After a while, when they have finished, they go away.

They say that the monkeys dig wild potatoes. They bring them to the river-bank. They roast them. The child will ask the mother, 'Mother, are they not roasted?' The mother will reply, 'They are not roasted yet.' The child will answer, 'Oh!' After a time the child will ask again, 'Mother, are they roasted yet?' The mother will reply, 'Not yet, my child'. After a time the monkeys take out their own potatoes and eat them.

They say that one day the monkeys whipped a Nuer man. They loosened the rope which was round his waist and whipped him with it. They chased him into the barn and went away.

They say that one day when the monkeys were drinking and throwing clods on the river-bank three big male monkeys were the last to go. A crocodile caught one. When they saw that one of them was caught they all threw themselves into the river. They dived, hunting for him. They rose to the surface together in the middle of the river. When they failed to find the captured monkey they came out. One of them cried. It may have been his brother or his wife. One male monkey went to comfort it as it threw itself again and again on the ground.

THE LION AND THE FOX

The lion was very hungry. He saw antelope at night and chased them. When he was near one he sprang upon it, but he fell into a deep well. He was in that well for many days. There was no way to get out of it. It was a slippery well. When he tried to get out he fell back. The lion was very much bewildered.

One day the fox came to the top of the well. He stopped. The lion asked him, 'Who are you?' He said, 'I am the fox.' The lion said, 'Oh! son of my sister, come to me.' The fox looked into the well. He said to the lion, 'How did you fall into the well?' The lion said to him, 'I was springing upon an antelope.' He said to the fox, 'Son of my sister, come to me.' The fox said to him, 'How would I get you out, uncle? Would not I fall in?' The lion said, 'I would take hold of your foot.' The fox refused. He went away.

A monkey came. He stopped at the top of the well. 'Who are you?' called the lion. 'I am a monkey,' he replied. The lion said, 'Come to me, son of my sister.' The monkey refused.

The fox heard their conversation. He called the monkey and said to him, 'You help the uncle of a person out.' The monkey was surprised, but he said to the lion, 'How will you get out?' The lion said to him, 'I will take hold of your foot.'

The monkey went down. The lion caught hold of his foot. They came out. Then the monkey said, 'Let go my foot; let us travel. I brought you out, uncle.' The lion said to the monkey, 'I am starved to death. I will eat you, son of my sister. I am absolutely famished. Maybe my body will then be strong! The monkey said, 'Why! Uncle! What! But I brought you out!'

The fox heard their conversation. He did not come near. His words were from a distance. He and the monkey made a plan. He said to the monkey, 'You let the uncle of a person eat you.' He said to the lion, 'The people of the village are resting after work. We will go under the tree in the shade.' The lion came, bringing the monkey with him. They talked. The fox said to the monkey, 'Let the lion eat you. The uncle of a person is utterly famished. But one always eats a monkey in a tree.' The monkey heard the words of the fox gladly. With a spring he was in the top of the tree. The lion was left on the ground. The fox fled.

The lion cried on the ground under the tree; he cried as he went away.

THE FOX AND HIS MOTHER

A long time ago the fox and his mother had a village. The fox often went fishing. In the afternoon he would come home with his catch. He would put the fish on the ground. He would say to his mother, 'Prepare this catch of fish; you cook it.' The mother would prepare the fish and the fox would eat it. The same thing would happen next day. When the fish were cooked he would say to his mother, 'Bring me all the fish and the head and the neck. Bring it all.' The mother would give him all. He ate it. He would leave his mother out.

This went on for a month. He himself ate all the fish. He went fishing, brought his catch home and said to his mother, 'Mother, why is the tail of the fish like this? Bring the other parts and the head and the neck and the gravy. Bring all of it, mother.'

The mother was very thin, resembling a certain very thin fish. When he had finished eating he would call to his mother, 'Mother, mother-of-the-fox, bring water. Your son has had enough.' The mother would hiss. The fox would hear. The fox would say, 'What, mother-of-the-fox, did you hiss at your child?' The mother would say, 'Nothing, my son.' She would go to the river. She would give him the water.

When the mother grew very thin, she went to a woman

called Nyajwani. Nyajwani knew how to plan all kinds of things. The mother-of-the-fox said to Nyajwani, 'My sister, my child is killing me. My son has no consideration. Show me what to do.' Nyajwani said to her, 'Go to the forest. Bring gum from the tree. I will show you a plan. You will surely be healthy after to-day.'

Mother-of-the-fox brought the gum. She gave it to Nyajwani. Nyajwani formed a very nice woman, a very red woman, she put beads in her ears and she put anklets on her legs also. She made her out of gum. She was a very good woman who had never had children yet. When she was finished Nyajwani created a name for her. She called her Nyaluac.

That day the fox went fishing. They gave Nyaluac to the mother-of-the-fox. The mother brought her to the house. She spread a mat and put her sitting on it. In the afternoon the fox brought in fish. He threw them on the ground and called his mother. 'Mother-of-the-fox, cut up that catch of fish.' His mother said to him, 'Oh, my son, there is a traveller at the village, a woman who refuses to live with her husband. She says "My husband is the fox!"' The fox exclaimed, 'I told you to hurry with the fish so that the guest may eat.' His mother answered, 'Oh!' She roasted the catch of fish. She offered it to the fox. The fox refused. He said to his mother, 'I know, mother-of-the-fox, that I am ashamed to eat in front of my sweetheart. Give the fish to the guest.' Mother-of-the fox brought the food into the house and ate it herself. Every time fish was cooked she offered it to the fox, but he refused to have it. Mother-of-the-fox brought it again into the house. Mother-of-the-fox ate it.

Mother-of-the-fox got so fat that her skin was very smooth. When she knew that she was fat she said to the fox, 'My son, to-day you and your wife may visit. I will tell you one thing, my son. Do not whip the daughter of the Nuer. This one has a very tender skin. Do not harm her.' The fox answered. 'Oh!'

Late that afternoon the fox went to the house. When he went into the house he said to Nyaluac, 'Blow the fire.' She was silent. The fox said, 'I will blow the fire in the house of my mother.' When he had blown the fire he said to the woman, 'What is it?' She was silent still.

He pushed her with his club. The club stuck. He tried to pull it back and thought that the woman perhaps had caught it. He said to her, 'Let my club alone.' The woman was silent. He said, 'What! Have you not heard that I always whip a guest? I am the fox.' He said again to the woman, 'Do you want to be whipped. Are you not a guest? Let go of my club.' The club fell of its own accord. He again pushed the woman with the club. 'What's the matter?' The club again stuck in the body of the woman.

The fox again said to Nyaluac, 'But why are you always holding my club? Let it alone, if you are really like the daughter of a man.' The woman was silent. The fox did not know that the woman was formed of gum. He took his raw-hide whip. He struck the woman across the back. Her back broke.

The fox fled.

THE FOX AND HIS BROTHER TUTLUET

The fox said to Tutluet, 'My brother, we will go and hunt us a cow.' His brother replied, 'O, yes.' They took their weapons. They started out. They arrived at a certain village and entered it. It was a village of the ogres. They went to the barn. Tutluet found a cow. He called the fox, 'Come, here is our cow.' The fox replied,

'Brother, that is not our cow. But come.' Tutluet came, but that cow was an ogre.

They started out. Tutluet led the cow while the fox drove it. The sky was clouded. The clouds opened. The fox saw the anger of the ogre. Tutluet said, 'My brother, I will come. Drive our cow.' While Tutluet led the cow the fox stole away.

When the ogre was worn out, he asked Tutluet, 'A while ago, when you came and brought me away, did you know whether I was a cow or a wild animal?'

Tutluet fled. He tripped and fell. The ogre caught him. He said to Tutluet, 'No, I will not eat you. But it is different with your brother. I will hunt for his body, that fox.'

The fox meantime hurried to the village and began to play the fiddle in his house. The ogre came to the door. 'Village of mother-of-the-fox,' he called, 'I am waiting at your house.' The fox knew his voice. He said to his mother, 'Mother, what shall we do?' His mother replied, 'My son, what shall we do?' He said to his mother, 'Put me in the big gourd.' His mother said, 'Can you get in?' He said to his mother, 'I can get in.' They hung the gourd up high.

The ogre waited outside the house. He asked mother-of-the-fox, 'Where is the fox?' Mother-of-the-fox said to him, 'Where could he be here in the house?' The ogre said to her, 'Who played the fiddle? Did you know how to play the fiddle long ago?' Mother-of-the-fox said, 'If the fox came into this house there is no place where he could hide himself.' The ogre said, 'Tell me at once where he is.' Mother-of-the-fox replied, 'I do not know.'

The ogre said to mother-of-the-fox, 'I will not leave without a gift in my hand. What is in that gourd?' Mother-of-the-fox said, 'Beans which I will plant in the spring.' The ogre said, 'Is it full?' She said, 'It is full.' Mother-of-the-fox hesitated. The ogre exclaimed, 'No, give it to me at once.' She stood up. She gave it to him.

The ogre left. He talked to himself as he went along the path. 'That god of the village of mother-of-the-fox! Why! I left empty-handed without finding a thing.' The fox spoke. 'Where are you taking the gourd which belongs to the village of mother-of-the-fox? Let it down to the ground slowly.'

The ogre exclaimed, 'God, wait. I will let it down slowly.' He put it down and fled.

Then the fox exclaimed, 'Let us each catch a person.' They turned back to back. The fox ran to his village and the ogre to the ogres. The fox said, 'You, ogre, measured yourself against me. Did you find my cleverness?'

RIDDLES

1. Guess what are the red dates which are in the sky but never fall?
    (*Answer*) They are stars.
2. Guess what tree it is which stands in the middle of the river but never goes under the water?
    (*Answer*) It is a lotus.
3. Guess what is a fat woman?
    (*Answer*) It is a window.
4. Guess what is a red hornless cow but its horns are of skin?
    (*Answer*) It is a dog.
5. Guess what tree it is that has many hands but never climbs?
    (*Answer*) It is kaffir corn.
6. Guess a red thing which carries its horn?
    (*Answer*) It is a scorpion.

7. Guess what big girl it is who has a dancing skirt but never goes to a dance?
   (*Answer*) It is a house. (The Nuer house has long grass eaves, crudely resembling the grass dancing skirt.)
8. Guess what big man it is near whom they have the wedding talk but he never makes a remark?
   (*Answer*) It is a barn. (The wedding talk is often staged near the barn.)
9. Guess what two males it is that hold their father?
   (*Answer*) They are pillars (supporting the barn).
10. Guess what forest it is which one may cut down but it is never finished?
    (*Answer*) It is the hair.
11. Guess what death it is where they never have the ceremony of terminating the period of mourning?
    (*Answer*) It is sleep.
12. Guess what it is which one holds but it will never overcome a person?
    (*Answer*) Kaffir corn which has been sifted. (The sifting process is called 'holding it'.)
13. Guess what are two big males which will never meet?
    (*Answer*) The clouds and the earth.
14. Guess what are two big rugs?
    (*Answer*) They are the sky and the earth.
15. Guess two big males?
    (*Answer*) They are the banks of the river.
16. Guess the crocodile which cries?
    (*Answer*) It is a (native made) fiddle.

INDEX

Animals, ix, 11, 12, 14, 20, 23-4, 56; in folk-lore: dog, 82, 88-9, 90; rats, 90; crocodile, 94-6; elephant, 95; frog, 96-7; monkeys, 97-8, 99-100; lion, 98-9; fox, 98-9, 100-4. *See also* Cattle.

Birds, 92-3, 96.
Burial rites, ix, 52-4, 56.

Cattle: Nuer pride in, vii, 11-12, 25; care of, in sickness, 12, 25; fear of cows without horns, 11-12; at the fishing camp, 12; moved in search of pasture, viii, x; protective prayer, x-xi; see new moon, 12, 82; seldom eaten, 14; offered as sacrifice, x, 14; cattle as marriage price, 27-8, 36-9, 40-1, 60, 67; boy with unhealed tribal marks may not tend, 32; game with cattle, 66-7; cattle raids, 71, 74; taken for taxes, 73; in folk-lore, 90, 91-2, 94, 102-3.
Characteristics of Nuer, v, vii, xi, 62-5.
Childbirth and after, x, 10, 42-5.
Climate, 79, 83.

Dancing, 67-8, 25; dance skirt, 5; girl begins going to, 27; courtship in fishing camp, 37; wedding dance, 38, 40; war dance, 71.
Death, 52-5.
Diseases, prevalent, 28, 47-52.
District Commissioners, 3, 17, 25, 48-9; decisions of, respected, 73-4; employs Nuer, 75; favourite official murdered, 74.

Employment, native trades, 16; paid work, 17.
Evil eye: dread of, 58; precautions against, 10, 30, 34, 44, 50, 51.

Fishing, vii; fishing season, 12-13, 25, 37, 43, 83; folk-lore, 100-2.

Folk-lore, vii, 88-104.

Games, 26, 65-9.
Government, relations with, v, 73; cotton introduced by, 16; Nuer used as interpreters, 17; contacts with officials, 25; used as medical helpers, 48; conflict over raids, 71; punitive patrols, 72, 75; use of aeroplanes, 72-5; taxes, 48, 73-4; educative and medical aid, 28, 48-9, 73-5.

Heavenly bodies, 73, 82-3.

Language, the Nuer: affinities of, vi; study of, v, 80-1; Language Conference at Rejaf, vii, 1, 78, 81; books in, 81; distinctive points in, 81-2; divisions of time, 82-5; names and relationships 84-5; greetings 86-7.

Marriage: preparation of girls for, 26-8, 37-8; male authority, 27-8; marriage price, 36, 37; courting at the fishing camp, 37; the marriage talk, 37-8; if the bride objects, 38-9; the wedding dance, 40; married woman's garb, 41; the feast and after, 41; customs concerning marriage, 41-2; breaking an engagement, 59-60; divorce, 60-1; a curious case, 61.
Measuring, method of, 69-70.
Medical work: Government, 28, 47-9, 74; by the mission, 28, 48, 58, 75-7.
Medicine men (sorcerer), x, 3, 51-2.
Mission, account of work, 75-9.
Moral code of Nuer, 58-61.
Music, Nuer, 24, 68-9.

Nuer tribe, the: origin, vii, 1-2; habitat, vi-vii, 1; tribal subdivisions, vii, 1; physical type, vi-vii, 2-3; raids, vii, 71; clothing, 3-5; food, 13-16; the

108 INDEX

house and its furnishing, viii, 19–21; a woman's day, 21–5; a man's work, 25; Nuer children, 26; the girl, 26–8; the boy and his tribal marks, 29–35; diseases, 47–52; death and burial, 52–5; religion and superstition, viii–xi, 56–8; Nuer moral law, 58–61; games, 65–9; wider relations of Nuer, 71–9; folk-lore, 86–104. *See also* Cattle, Marriage, Ornaments, Women.

Ogre, 11–12, 26, 82; in folk-lore, 88, 93–4, 102–4.
Ornaments: fashions in beads, 8; ornaments of men, 6–8, 32; of women, 8–9, 44–5; of girls, 9–10, 27; of babies and children, 10, 43, 44; the bride's ornaments, 36–40, 41; at the wedding dance, 40; at time of burial, 53–4; during and after mourning, 54–5; protective beads, 58; ornaments in games, 66.

Religion: Nuer gods, viii, 56–7, 72–3; a legend of Kot, viii–ix; some Nuer prayers, ix–xi; influence of Christianity, 34, 57, 63, 64–5, 77–8.
Riddles, 26, 69, 104–5.

Schools for Nuer, 75, 77–8.
Sexual relations, 26, 58–61.
Snakes, 11, 52; in folk-lore, ix, 88–9, 90–3.

Tribal marks: details of the rite, 29–32, 34; effect on status, 33; Ox name assumed, 12; system of class-names, 33; given to one woman, 34; an albino, 34–5.
Tribes, neighbouring, v–vi, 71, 76–7.
Twins, 45–6, 85.

Weapons: spears and clubs, 13, 16, 20, 21, 25, 51, 54; guns scarce, 14, 74.
Women and girls: appearance, 3, 5; clothing, 4–5; ornaments, 8, 20; milk as food, 14; pounding the dura, 15; making pottery, 16; decorating gourds, 69; sleeping place and pillow, 19, 29; bringing in fuel, 21; a day's work, 21–4; grandmothers and babies, 26; as the girl grows up, 26–8; at the cutting of tribal marks, 30, 32, 33, 34; courtship and marriage, 36–42; desire for children, 42; childbirth, x, 42–3; mother and baby, 43–5; mother and twins, 45–6; an incredible tale, 46; medicine women, 51–2; mourning for a woman, 54; some superstitions, 7, 57–8; the moral code, 59–61; a woman with 'wives', 61; girls' games, 67–8; to ascertain a woman's age, 85; terms of respect, 87; in folk-lore, 90–3, 93–4, 100–2.

56141
DT
13.2
.H8
1970